CW00557807

Also by Trevor Pateman

The Best I Can Do

Materials and Medium: An Aesthetics

Silence Is So Accurate

Studies in Pragmatics

All published by **degree zero**

Trevor Pateman

Prose Improvements

degree zero

First published 2017 by **degree zero**
Unit 10, 91 Western Road, Brighton BN1 2NW, England
degreezeropublisher@gmail.com

ISBN 978-0-9935879-4-8

2 4 6 5 3 1

A CIP catalogue record for this book is available
from the British Library

Printed and Bound by CPI Group (UK) Ltd, Croydon CR0 4YY

FSC
www.fsc.org
MIX
Paper from
responsible sources
FSC® C013604

Prose Improvements

This book is from a first edition
of five hundred numbered copies.
This is Number

29

Each copy is signed by the author
on the title page.

Contents

Introduction

Part One

Part Two

Part Three

Work in Progress

Introduction

On Language in General

LANGUAGE spreads like the plague, carried by every instance of speech. It finds in human beings a receptive culture for its replication and mutation. Language and human beings are made for each other. But human beings as social actors and societies as organisations of power devote considerable cognitive and material resources to its control – to its monitoring and institutionalisation. Language is rarely allowed to go its own way. Individuals modify their speech to fit what they think are the prevailing prestige norms, though they often get it wrong. Governments order the standardisation of national languages, spoken and written. This labour of Sisyphus is assigned to teachers who may not be inquisitive about the complexity of language and who may see their task as involving primarily the repression of stigmatized forms. They teach children to not split infinitives, deaf to the epidemic of linguistic change raging in the playground.

Language is natural to humans; like seeing, we do it extremely well – and, in large measure, this is because we do not do it at all. At the beginning of life, it is something to which we are liable, rather than something of which we are capable. We become language users without knowing how, acquiring competences which are some of the most complex of our lives. Later on, what language does to us and what we can do with language become for some people the most fascinating things in the world.

All things change says Heraclitus. Language is among those things and change is its natural state. Cultural dams cannot stand out against the tides: we cannot build enough of them, fast enough; nor do we fully understand how and where to build them. *Language change is irresistible* and any understanding of the place of language in human worlds must begin by reckoning with that.

Communication in language comes very easily to humans, and idiolects and dialects with significant differences can be mutually intelligible. The correction in which we engage is mostly unnecessary to communication – indeed it presupposes it, since otherwise we would not know what to correct. Correction is surplus to the needs of communication. It is an example of what in another context Herbert Marcuse called "surplus repression". It is a study in itself to understand the motivations of activities which aim at language maintenance, a study that has to look at the building of identity, the drive to discriminate, the consolidation of cultural power, and at obsession and paranoia.

How language works and how we believe it works or ought to work are different orders of reality between which we are constantly buffeted. My starting position is that those who lay down language rules inhabit junk shops where what is true and what they would like to be true are all jumbled up. This gives me some confidence to pick and choose my own rules. Of course, I thereby lay myself open to correction and the self-inflicted title of this book makes it a sitting duck for anyone in possession of a musket. So too does the fact that I do my own copy-editing to ensure that whatever wilfulness there is in my prose survives through to what you are now reading. I concede only that I have not blocked the modern Sisyphus which tirelessly pushes out red, green and blue wriggles, though many are simply told to go away. (In an Introduction, when one is still at the stage of trying to win over the reader, one should write diplomatically).

Prose is normally written out of larger purposes than proseing for the sake of it. Chapters 1, 2 and 3 try to exemplify that truth. But larger purposes are unknown to language obsessives, who will always be with us and have parts in the casts of chapters 4 through 8 where I try to obsess with the rest. On a larger stage, language nationalists erect fantastic borders to interrupt the free-flow of communication. I discuss their efforts in chapter 9. These thumb-nailed chapters make up Part One.

Part Two is more academic in style. In chapters 10 and 11 there is a general intellectual debt to Freud. It would have been wonderful to have met him, best of all in the way inveigled by Franz in Robert Seethaler's *The Tobacconist*. Franz has the excellent good sense to offer Freud fine cigars (most likely pilfered) in exchange for practical advice on conducting a love life. Smart boy. I did have the chance to meet Jacques Lacan, whose early work I make use of in chapter 11. *Votre lettre m'intéresse* he wrote, inviting me to contact his secretary. I had sent him a carefully composed letter on arrival in Paris, when my French was still rudimentary, but then found myself unable to imagine what I might say in person - *il fait beau temps?* - and flunked the opportunity. The gossip had already told me Lacan's preferred cigars, but I was no Franz.

I did get to shake hands with Noam Chomsky and was able to thank him for extensive help with earlier drafts of the book I handed him, my *Language in Mind and Language in Society*. That book developed the leading (and fundamentally Chomskyan) ideas re-presented here in chapter 12 but which are also more diffusely present throughout this book, including in the opening paragraphs of this introduction. Chapter 12 starts quite technically, and insists on distinctions where there is often confusion - as when I prise apart *intuition* from *judgement* - but it aims at a very general conclusion.

I would be happy to owe something to the digressive style of Roland Barthes, whose seminars provided binary opposition to the intolerable monologues of other professors. When I sent him a copy of my intransigent first book, Barthes thanked me for my *pensée fidèle* but since the thanks were on the back of a holiday postcard showing surfers at Biarritz, I suspect some irony. This book tries to be closer in spirit even when it is critical of the letter. There is hopefully some pleasure to be derived from the texts which make up the non-academic chapters of Part Three, not that you should fast forward to them right now.

In an Introduction, one should reassure the reader that what follows all hangs together. I would be surprised if it did. I defy anyone to live to seventy and show no signs of self-contradiction. The real contradictions of the world are enough to make all of us at odds with ourselves.

Part One

1

Making It Up As You Go Along

WE are not taught to speak but we are taught to write. With speaking, listening to other people triggers our ability and we start to join in as best we can. With writing, we first of all learn some formulas and only later get to know enough to discard them.

Once upon a time in my country, a child who had just learnt to write acquired at the same time an important obligation. *Dear Auntie, Thank you for my birthday present. It is very nice. I had a nice birthday. Mummy says we will see you soon. Love ...* Time passes and the obligation does not become less burdensome but its fulfilment becomes a little more varied. *Dear Auntie, Thank you for my birthday present. The pom-pom hat is very nice. Now I have three pom-pom hats. I had a nice birthday with my friends. We went to the zoo. Mummy sends her love. Love ...*

Eventually, if we are lucky, we learn to make it up as we go along just as we do when we are speaking, and the writing formulas - if they do not disappear entirely - become less visible. We improvise on forms which were laid down in our earliest years and the improvisations may take us a long way from the original starting point.

Unless we are going to remain stuck in childhood, we have to do that. Becoming a competent writer just is about making it up as you go along. But that is also to say that you *think* as you go along, you *imagine* as you go along, you *feel* as you go along - and for many things you are

17

unlikely to think or imagine or feel them unless you are writing. Writing is a means of producing thoughts or, more severely, writing is the produced means for the production of thoughts, images, feelings. A novelist may have an idea for a character before sitting down to write but the character only emerges in the writing, just as a portrait of someone only emerges in the painting. Oh, agreed, the painter may have an idea how you should sit, how you should turn your head, and so on - that's the formula at work - but there is no portrait without paint and the paint goes on bit by bit. As with the character in the portrait, the character in the novel emerges in real time.

The fact that we make things up as we go along in real time explains the need for revision. When we are busy tripping along, painting the face or telling the story, we simply can't keep our eyes or our minds on everything at once. To a degree, we are distracted by our own thoughts and feelings triggered in the painting or the writing. So we have to go back, clean up a bit of background, tidy up a line and oil a transition. If you are impatient or lazy, going back over your work will feel frustrating. Why can't I get on with something new? And if you are modest, looking over your own work will seem a bit narcissistic. In that case, you need to get into the habit of looking at your first version as if it was the work of someone else, looking at it with what we call a critical eye or listening with a critical ear. Sometimes, at least for writing, part of the task may be sub-contracted to someone else, an editor – for which I do not think there is really an equivalent in painting. But whether in relation to pictures or prose, going back is usually vital – going back and doing it over again can transform something from the passable to the more than passable.

So it took me maybe fifteen minutes to type out the first version of these opening paragraphs, starting with not much more than the title and making it up from there. But by the time you read this, it will have been fiddled with and touched up and even rebuilt and all that will have taken rather more than fifteen minutes, so that it's no longer true to say that I made it up as I went along. That's not to deny that on other occasions we may have no choice but to improvise …

*

It was a dark and stormy night but because it was Christmas Eve there were still people about, hurrying to complete last minute Christmas shopping. The brightly lit shop windows promised relief from the wet and windy weather outside. A girl and a man, obviously her father, stood peering into a bookshop window, the collars of their coats turned up against the wind and rain. The man pointed to a book in the window.

"Look, Rita, there's the new Janet and Allan Ahlberg, *It was a Dark and Stormy Night*. I'd really like to read that. But it's in hardback. I can't afford it now after all the shopping we've done, and anyway it will come out in paperback after Christmas."

Rita said nothing.

"Come on," said her father, "We must be getting home."

He took her hand and they walked off together, their heads turned down against the rain. Rita looked up at her father.

"What do you think the story is about? Do you think it's a Christmas story?"

"Not with a title like that. Mind you, I can't say what

I think it would be about. *It was a Dark and Stormy Night*. Well, it could be about anything."

"Yes, but what do you *guess* it's about?" persisted Rita.

At this moment, father and daughter reached their car. Rita got into the front passenger seat, and her father went round and let himself in to the driver's side. He switched on the engine and the car lights. Rita loved the glow of the dashboard lights, especially on such a dark and stormy night. She imagined that it was a sort of fireside, and she snuggled up in her seat as the car moved off, swishing its way along the wet streets.

"Go on, Dad, what is it about? Have a guess!"

After a pause, her father replied, "I think it goes like this ...

It was a dark and stormy night and the four bears were sitting round a blazing log fire in their little cottage deep in the middle of the Enchanted Wood. 'Tell us a story, Grumpy!' exclaimed Baby Bear, looking at the big old grizzly bear sitting nearest the fire whose name, of course, was Grumpy. He sometimes gets left out of stories about the bears, which is quite wrong because there were really four bears not three, though I never make the mistake of leaving him out.

Rita's father glanced towards his daughter, who put on a furious look.

"Dad, don't tease. Tell me what you really think it's about."

"I am," said her father, putting on a shocked look, "And the story goes on like this, I'm quite sure ...

Grumpy looked grumpy. 'Children, children,' he sighed, 'Always wanting stories. Never content. Can't amuse themselves these days. Way they're brought up. Different in my day. Had to amuse ourselves.' And he would have gone on like that for several minutes had not

Baby Bear's mother intervened and scolded, 'Oh, come on, Grumpy, tell us a story. It's a dark and stormy night, we're all sitting comfortably around the fire and you do tell such good stories.' Grumpy was obviously delighted by this last remark. His grumpy face softened, and he replied, 'Oh, very well then. Just one. And not a long one.' The other three bears sat patiently and waited, until Grumpy began:

"It was a dark and stormy night, but because it was Christmas Eve, there were still people about hurrying to complete last minute Christmas shopping. The brightly lit shop windows promised relief from the wet and windy weather outside.

A girl and a man, obviously her father, stood peering into a bookshop window, the collars of their coats turned up against the wind and rain. The man pointed to a book in the window..."

Rita interrupted, banging on the dashboard:

"Dad, if this is going to be a story about us, I'm not listening. Why can't you tell stories about other people? I'd even listen to stories about princes and princesses!"

"Just a minute, just a minute!" protested her father, "You don't know what comes next."

"What does come next?"

"This is what comes next ...

Suddenly, Grumpy stopped in mid-sentence, looked at the other bears, and said, 'No, I don't think I'm going to tell that story tonight. It's too scary on a dark and stormy night. I'm going to tell you a different one.' And he paused, cleared his throat and began again:

"Once upon a time, it was a warm and sunny day, and the eighteen bears decided to go for a walk before breakfast..."

'What!' exclaimed Baby Bear, 'You can't have a story with eighteen bears in it, it's against the rules!'

Before Grumpy could reply, Baby Bear's father interrupted, 'Now, now, Baby Bear, just listen. There aren't any rules as far as stories go, except that they have a beginning, middle and end. Now just settle down and listen to Grumpy.' And he nodded towards Grumpy to continue the story.

'Thank you,' said Grumpy, and continued ...

"These eighteen bears lived together in a cottage deep in the middle of the Enchanted Wood and their names were..." - here Grumpy drew a very deep breath - "Allan, Betty, Colin, Dinah, Esmerelda, Flossie, Giorgio, Horace, Ian, Janet, Kitty, Loretta, Maurice, Nadia, Obadiah, Peter, Roy and Shirley..."

At this point, Baby Bear interrupted and wailed, 'How am I supposed to remember all those names? I'm only a Baby Bear. It's not fair. It must be against the rules...' - Baby Bear looked at his father - 'It must be against the rules to have so many names in a story that you can't remember them.'

And it looked as if Baby Bear was about to burst into tears. But Grumpy Bear smiled, and said ...

'But I'm sure you can remember them, Baby Bear. Did you notice they were in Alphabetical Order?'

'Yes,' said Baby Bear, shortly and grudgingly.

'Well, then,' said Grumpy, 'Let's go through them together. The first bear's name began with A for...'

And, sure enough, Baby Bear could remember all eighteen names and, after that, Grumpy Bear continued with his story...

"So the eighteen bears set out for a walk in the Enchanted Wood, walking in a crocodile with Allan in the front and..."

- here Grumpy paused and looked at Baby Bear, who smiled and cried, 'Shirley!' -

"And Shirley at the back of the crocodile. Now you may imagine" - continued Grumpy - *"that these eighteen bears were quite a peculiar sight, walking in a crocodile into the Enchanted Wood on a warm and sunny day. And when a little girl, who was also out for a walk, spotted them, she could scarcely believe her eyes and stood shocked still with amazement..."*

"Goldilocks?" interrupted Rita.

"Whatever makes you think she's Goldilocks?" replied her father. And looking over his glasses at Rita he said, "She's in the story with the THREE bears, isn't she?"

Rita was cross.

"Yes, but I can't see how it can be anyone else, even if there are eighteen bears. I think when Grumpy says she's a little girl out for a walk, you're meant to guess that she IS Goldilocks."

"I wouldn't be so sure," replied her father, "Because the story continues like this …

Baby Bear almost jumped out of his seat, 'It's Goldilocks!' he shouted. But Grumpy Bear looked at him in a puzzled way and asked, 'Whatever makes you think that? Goldilocks is in the story with the THREE bears, isn't she?'

'Yes, she is,' said Baby Bear, 'But she can be in this story too, can't she? It's not against the rules, is it?'

'No, it's not against the rules,' replied Grumpy, 'It's just that she isn't in this story. The little girl in this story is called Rita.'

Now this time Rita really did thump the dashboard.

"Dad, you know that I do not - repeat, DO NOT - like stories with me in them. Tell me a different story, PLEASE!"

But just at that moment the car came to a halt and Dad exclaimed:

"Home at last!"

Rita peered out of the window.

"Already? That didn't seem long."

"Of course it didn't," said Rita's father, "I've been telling you a story."

"No you haven't," snorted Rita, "It didn't have a beginning, a middle and end, just lots of beginnings."

"Are you sure?" said her father. "Anyway, let's not argue about it out here on such a dark and stormy night. Let's go in beside the fire."

So they did, and sat around the fire with Rita's Mum and her Grumpy Grandpa. And soon Rita found herself saying, "Tell us a story, Grandpa." And Grandpa, after huffing and puffing a bit, began to tell a story, but he didn't get very far before Rita threw a cushion at him, which may not seem a very nice thing to do. But you see, Grandpa's story just happened to start like this ...

"It was a dark and stormy night ... "

*

In the high period of Protestant religious belief, life's journey was not complete without a crisis of faith. There came a point for every serious believer when they realised that they had inherited their beliefs from their family and milieu, and that the same influences which made them a Protestant on this side of the mountains would have made them a Catholic on the other. So how could you be sure that yours were the true beliefs? The crisis of faith thus precipitated could be long-lasting and was the central subject of published spiritual autobiographies, troubled narratives where all ended well. The crisis resolved itself and you emerged from it able to speak your beliefs in your own voice, with your own conviction, no longer simply a *porte-parole* for what you had inherited. You became fluent in your religion and accented it in your own way. If you wrote about it, the writing was no longer cut and paste.

You become fluent in a theory, fluent in a style, in pretty much the same way that you become fluent in a second language. You have to work at it, sometimes over an extended period of time, you have to practice a lot, and you must have at least a bit of talent. Leave it too late in life, and you will never get to be fluent in a new language. Ability to develop theories and styles perhaps does not have a clear lifetime cut-off point, but it certainly helps to start early. But equally important is the sort of confidence which allows you to step out in your own words even when some of them may be the wrong words. You become fluent in your religion or a new language by making mistakes along the way. It's unlikely that you first succeed; usually you have to try again and sometimes again and again. There is no end to making it up.

2

Playing a Bad Hand Well

THE story of late Matisse is familiar: confined to his bed
or a wheelchair following surgeries for cancer, he
largely gave up painting and for the last part of his life
(1941 – 1954) used scissors to cut up gouache-painted
paper. His assistants painted the paper, they pinned up
the cut-outs, re-arranged them according to his instruc-
tions, and finally glued the cut-outs to their backing
board. Many of the works were large-scale, but not all.
We look at them individually now, but Matisse was
surrounded by them in a studio which they made bright
and colourful. His place of work and its contents were
always important to Matisse; there is now a book about
that, *Matisse in the Studio*, the companion to an exhibition on the subject.

It's a commonplace that some artists produce really
good work when they are old and handicapped by poor
eyesight, shaky hands, limited ability to move around,
loss of strength and range in their voice (think of Leonard
Cohen's final album *You Want It Darker*). It's as if they
have been dealt a bad hand but manage to play it very
well. Of course, they carry into the game all the knowledge and know-how they have accumulated over their
lifetimes and that's probably a large part of what enables
them to turn in a late performance which may range from
the simply decent to the magnificent. Jean Rhys was
seventy-six when her splendid *Wide Sargasso Sea* was
published in 1966, her publisher taking a gamble in trying

to bring back to literary life someone whose earlier work was more or less forgotten.

Limitations due to age or infirmity are not always a handicap but can function as a sort of formal device which challenges someone to do the best work they can. In poetry, if forms like the haiku or the sonnet were merely restrictions on what is and isn't allowed, they would have little popularity. But they are not just restrictions; they are able to set off imaginative, creative responses which either bring out the best in the form or, as it were, over-ride the constraints of the form – so that we barely notice that we are reading a haiku or a sonnet. When we look at Matisse's late work, we don't need to know that he was working under practical constraints. We don't need to excuse the shortcomings in the work – *pity he had to make do with cut-outs.* The late works succeed in and for themselves, the results of a hand played exceptionally well. The bad hand forced the development of a formal device which, as it turned out, yielded a style which could house a vision. The device was liberating rather than constraining. That is why we don't pity Matissse for having to fall back on it.

*

After the War (the First), my mother's sister Winnie married a tall dark handsome man called Jack Burke. Uncle Jack worked at Eynsford Paper Mill on the River Darenth until the mill closed in 1952. The mill produced hand-made paper of a quality to make even the best modern Bond Street stuff look banal. Jack was a paper maker and kept samples of his work and, in his retirement, showed me them. Rub your thumb down the edges and you would have blood everywhere. Hold them up to the light and you saw watermarks fit for a king. Eventually he gave me a quire and after his death I used the sheets sparingly, only for love letters.

Uncle Jack explained how the paper was made and how "hand-made" really did mean that. And he went on to tell me that men who had shaken pulp into paper shaped by the deckle that gave the paper its edge – that those men would arrive at the mill one day, clocking in for the many thousandth time, and find that they could no longer shake the mould in the way they had done without thinking and over decades. You could lose your touch just like that and when it happened there was no disguising the fact that the pulp was all lumpy and shake as you might, the lumps remained. There was no role for men with the wrong shake in their hands.

The idea of a papermaker who wakes one day to find he has lost his touch always stayed with me. It's how I worry about this prose business. It gets harder and I keep seeing sentences which use a word deployed only a line ago and that's not what I reckon my style. I'm conservative about repetition unless it's very deliberate, like a note played three times. I have to keep going back over myself to check that the prose flows how it's meant and isn't all lumpy.

3

I Can Write It and
You Can Rhyme It

MANY years ago I travelled to Orkney, off the north coast of Scotland. Artists and craftspeople living on the island tried to make a living selling work to tourists like me. A friend who lived there pointed to some watercolours of local landscapes on sale. He told me that over the years, the land at the bottom had gradually reduced to a thin line and the sky above had expanded. There was an economic motive: you could paint the sky quicker than the land. In addition, it was generally believed that the artist had taught his wife how to do the sky and so now the watercolours were the work of two hands though still signed by just one. Husband and wife had created a price-competitive cottage industry which nicely illustrated Adam Smith's claims about the benefits of division of labour.

There are many works of art which are the work of more than one hand. In opera, the music is usually composed by someone whose name we know and the libretto written by someone whose name we don't, since it is never prominent on the advertising. That's partly because the libretto doesn't matter very much (it's usually a poor thing, laid out on a printed page) but partly also because we generally prefer to link our works of art to a single artist. We do so even for films which are credited to the director. A whole theory of film, *auteurism*, was invented decades ago to justify our inclinations. But it is a preference which also opens the way to outright abuse.

There are popular novelists who can only sustain the volume of output expected of them if, in whole or in part, they sub-contract the writing to other hands. The brand author may sign off the work as suitable for publication under their name but may have had really very little to do with the product's creation. The author's name on the book is then just like a designer label on a piece of clothing.

Readers of novels generally expect better than that and with good reason. A novel can only do what we want it to do if it is the work of one hand, no sub-contracting at all of the writing though there may be some delegation to assistants who provide historical and scientific detail or editorial feedback. But what is it that we want a novel to do that, give or take these bits, requires just one person's exclusive attention?

Novelists are expected to produce both the subject of the novel and do the telling, and one main reason why these tasks have to be held in one pair of hands is that the subject and the telling influence each other. Even if you have a detailed plot summary before you start work writing, the plot is unlikely to survive unchanged, uninflected, by the writing out of it. Additionally, it is not as if there is a standardised way of telling which would allow a plot summary to be handed over to a wordsmith to convert into a final version. That might be possible if instead of the novel form we had just one formula for the telling, which specified how to write a beginning, a middle and an end, most likely in that order. But novels as we now know them have freed themselves entirely from restrictive wordsmithing formulas which might encourage the idea that I can write it and you can rhyme it.

Writing is an experience in which the writer is constantly receiving feedback from the words which form on the page or on the screen and are heard (more or less clearly) in the writer's head. All the time, these words forming in front of one have to be accepted or rejected. In addition, they can't be stopped from setting off chains of thought or moments of emotion. The novelist is inevitably a reader of their own novel and that reader may get ideas into their head about what should happen next and how so-and-so would react in this situation, and so on indefinitely. As a result, the plot constructed in advance becomes a palimpsest where new plots are written over old ones, sometimes continuously.

This is all to the good because it pulls the novel away from the fate of being just a rather boring vehicle for some ideas which the writer has all worked out in advance and could have told you about over lunch. In writing a novel, a writer is pushed and pulled about all over the place; the reader of the finished version usually benefits from that. With any luck, they get to read a work where someone has been made to do some (fresh) thinking and some (fresh) feeling. The other side of this is that the business of writing is often experienced as hard work or frustrating or disturbing. It is much easier to write doggerel verse but, unfortunately, the market for that is limited to the quaint greetings card companies which still buy it.

*

There are various ways of developing the ideas of the preceding paragraphs. The novelist Milan Kundera sets out one way in *L'Art du Roman* where he ends up defining the novel as

> *La grande forme de la prose où l'auteur, à travers des egos expérimentaux (personnages), examine*

jusqu'au bout quelques grandes thèmes de l'existence
The great prose form where the author, by means of experimental egos (characters), examines to the limit some of the grand themes of life

This is unusual because it claims that the materials with which the novelist specifically works are *characters* which allow one to explore what might otherwise be called a story or a plot but is here called an examination. One might say that each of the traditional and great art forms has its own specific *Thing Good to Think With* (Lévi-Strauss's *chose bonne à penser*) – or perhaps more accurately, *Good to Express With*. For the potter, it is clay. For the sculptor, stone or metal. For the composer, sound and silence. And if Kundera is right, then for the novelist it is not words but *characters*.

When novelists work with characters, they have the chance to discover and bring into some kind of focus ways of human being and possibilities of human existence which would have eluded discovery or expression in mere prose. The characters need not be larger than life, though often they are, but they become larger than the idea a writer had about them before starting to write them into a novel. When an author has explored a character and allowed the character to expand and change, like a pot forming on the wheel, I think you can feel it and it's one of the things that keep you reading. I suppose that's more or less saying that the novel always tends towards a *Bildungsroman,* classically a novel of character formation, of growth and development. Kundera removes the chronological aspect of the typical *Bildungsroman* which takes us from childhood to adulthood and subsumes the genre within his *grande forme* where characters are pushed to their limits: limits of evil, limits of love, and many other possibilities. Among recent novels, Ottessa Moshfegh's *Eileen* uses over two hundred pages to develop the character of a first-person narrator, almost pushing her down our throats, before allowing just forty pages to spin off a more conventional story-line and ending. It's a good exemplification of what Kundera has in mind.

But the fact that words are the medium in which the author has to do this pushing explains why there can be no division of labour. I can imagine and develop a character into a character of a novel only insofar as I can put everything into words and accept those words as the ones I want for the character I had in mind. Or, formulated another way, I write words which when I read them I am willing to accept as part of the character I am exploring or examining. It is this *engagement* between what I have in mind and what the words on the page feed back to me that definitively closes off the possibility that I could sub-contract part of the job to someone else. No one can fill in the details because there are no details to be filled in until they are written. The character is in the detail. Manners maketh man, but words maketh characters.

But then I think of something which seems to not quite fit with Kundera's main claim. There are characters in fiction who become emotionally significant to the reader either because of or despite the fact that they are very thinly sketched. In consequence, we are left to invest them with significance – though the author has almost certainly plotted that we should do so. I call these thin personnages *Rorschach characters*, after the ink-blots. They crop up fairly often. I found one recently in Sebastian Barry's *Days Without End* where he creates a child character, Winona, about whom we are told very little but whose welfare comes to concern us, as likewise it concerns the main characters of the novel. *Nothing bad must happen to Winona* – and so you (or at least, I) keep reading the novel to make sure that, indeed, nothing bad does happen to her, whoever she may be.

In Penelope Fitzgerald's historical novel *The Blue Flower*, based on the life of the poet Novalis, the object of the poet's desire is a child called Sophie. There's apparently not much to say about Sophie. Fitzgerald tries to open a gap between the reality of Sophie and the poet's Rorschach-like investment in her so that we can appreciate both of them. But still the reader (at least, this reader) hangs in with the story to find out what will happen to her, not him. Sophie dies and it matters; the man who desires her dies and it's just a fact even though he is the poet Novalis and she is just a girl who dies at fifteen.

Both characters, Winona and Sophie, are created out of some very deft strokes, artfully placed and each linked to a big character whose emotional core is examined, partly by means of these cyphers into which both the big characters and we the readers project so much.

4

Prose Improvements

THE worldwide English language publishing industry is not modest about its merits. The literary agencies boast about the talent they have spotted – though, it's true, many of them are happy to rest on their laurels; they are "closed for submissions". The publishers adopt a similar posture. Both branches of the industry are awash with readers, editors, directors, all designated to ensure that only the best thumps down on the bookshop table. Authors acknowledge, sometimes at great length, the help of these industry insiders together with the outsiders who are their friends, family and dog. So it ought not to happen, though it does, that authors aiming to recreate a specific historical period manage to go into print with rather obvious anachronisms. There are people who make a hobby out of spotting anachronisms in Hollywood films and TV dramas. There is a parallel hobby to be made out of the latest historical novels. I don't read many, but here are a couple of examples to encourage you.

Sarah Perry, author of *The Essex Serpent* (2016), knows her Victorian England well and rarely slips. Not one among her many pre-publication readers, however, picked her up on these:

a *first-class stamp* (p. 415), unknown to the Victorians proud of their classless system: for most of the period, penny for a letter and half-penny for a postcard;

An urban housing situation which is *unsustainable* (p. 282), a term which belongs in the literary gutter anyway;

and, finally, poor William Ewart Gladstone gadding about with *hookers* (p. 48) which though it had currency in nineteenth century America still sounds to me so wildly out of place in a book about Victorian England that surely I am wrong and Sarah Perry knows something that I don't. For most of us, the upright Mr Gladstone walked the streets in search of *fallen women* or *prostitutes.*

On the other side of the Atlantic, Suzanne Rindell in *The Other Typist* (2014), an interesting novel set in first-person 1920s Prohibition America, creates a credibly mad narrator who does however slip into anachronism rather too often. I was distracted by

white noise (p. 41), *people person* (56), *time-line* (58), *body language* (136), *segued* (137), *trendy* (144), *leveraged* (159), and a *prepubescent* for which I have lost the page reference.

Now it is the job of those who read your novel in draft and get their names in your Acknowledgments to point out things like this and it is the job of novelists to make sure they find at least one reader with the necessary ear. Forget about the Links and the Likes, get someone who has an ear for the period. Nor must you allow political correctness to turn you deaf, for it can lead you to put into the mouth of a 1920s typist:

I remember thinking at the time, aside from the

> *simple fact of our gender, we did not appear to have*
> *much in common* (p. 46).

Oh dear, what they did have in common in those days was their *sex* as any lady novelist of the period could have told you. It's possible, of course, that Rindell is trying to merge or confuse herself as author with her mad narrator and that the anachronisms are her clues to what she is doing. But I don't buy into that story I have just made up for her and which, in any case, is contradicted in an interview where Rindell speaks of reading 1920s *Vogue* magazines as "useful in getting things right."

Someone could create a nice little website which would simply report on the anachronisms and related howlers which get past all those people whose job it is to ensure that they don't.

*

I doubt that men of an age to have liver spots are among the intended readers of Jane Fallon's *Skeletons* (2014). Indeed, the book's leading Bad Guy is just such a man. Nonetheless, I read it right through (all 430 + pages) quite easily and wanting to find out how things would turn out. The story is one which provokes thought and the telling of it, witty and convincing. So there's a Reader's Recommendation. But Jane Fallon does need an editor who will save her from a couple of stylistic skeletons which should be put back in the cupboard. I offer myself as just that editor.

Written English as we have perfected it contains constructions which are not felicitous. If a speaker, call her Jen, says in real life *I have enough haddock* then many of us will have been drilled at school to render it in

indirect speech as *Jen said that she had enough haddock.*
Likewise, should Jen place her knife and fork together
and declare *I have had enough haddock* then a well-
brought up author will give us in indirect speech *Jen said
that she had had enough haddock.*

Anyone who out of deference to school teachers wrote
that into a novel would be inviting re-direction to some
more suitable occupation. Oh, it's grammatical and so
on. It's just awful stylistically and to be avoided at almost
all costs. And it can be avoided without changing the
meaning. You do it by dropping into a form of Free
Indirect Discourse which allows you to avoid a surfeit of
Hads. So Jane Fallon's *She tried to remember what they
had had in common when they first met* (p.276) can be
transformed into *She tried to remember what they had in
common when they first met*, which is minus one *had* but
otherwise unchanged. If you get a taste for this, and can
get past your inner disapproving grammar teacher, you
could go on to rid yourself not only of *Had hads* but even
of *Hads.* So instead of *In the morning, she had waited to
go downstairs for breakfast until* ... (p. 314) you write,
*In the morning, she waited to go downstairs for breakfast
until* ....

But this is not obligatory. One *Had* is inoffensive; two
suggests carelessness. Novelists discovered how to
subvert school grammar at least a hundred and fifty years
ago and have been doing it ever since. The first academic
study of the use of such subversive free indirect forms
was published in 1897 in a ponderous journal, the
Zeitschrift für romanische Philologie.

A similar strategy will also rid your text of annoying
that that constructions:

*Both she and her mother had always known that that
would be out of the question* (p. 207).

But deleting one *that* is, in contrast, not out of the question whatever your school taught you.

If I was doing this style check in order to provide the police with a forensic profile of the writer, I would conclude on the evidence of the material I have presented that Jane Fallon went to an all-girls English private school where they were *strict* about these things. When I then conduct the usual corroborative check, Google gives me St Bernard's Convent School, Slough, an all-girls selective - but not private - grammar school. Nearly right.

*

The problem does go deeper. Traditionally, the rules for indirect discourse which schools taught and in some places still teach were designed to exclude low forms of speech from polite writing, whether low because they were obscene or profane or low because of their class or race associations. Indirect speech functioned to clean up the language of others and make the prose world a Sunday School place where the representing language was kept at a safe distance from the language of those supposedly represented. Things have changed for the better, it is true, and an obvious example is provided by changes in American writing where black or other minority ethnic characters speak. In the 1930s, the Ivy League-educated black writer Zora Neale Hurston wrote in what linguists came to call Standard American English, but tried to represent the Black English Vernacular of her characters in a non-patronising way by making modest use of Free Indirect forms in novels like *Their Eyes Were Watching God* (1937). Jump to 1982 and Alice Walker in *The Color Purple* got round the whole problem by diverting to the device of the epistolary novel, where there is no rewriting of how her characters express themselves. Jump forward again and the writing of authors like Junot Diaz (*This Is How You Lose Her* 2012) and Paul Beatty (*The Sellout* 2015) is simply a riot of language varieties, freed from the school rules, so much so that a reader on the British side of the Atlantic may struggle to understand.

5

How To Do Things With Commas

I rarely consult a dictionary now and never a grammar, style book or punctuation guide. Nor am I keen to let Microsoft Word do the job for me, and I concede with bad grace. This has to be childishness or cussedness or even a phobia but, as is often the case in such situations, I'd prefer to make the best of an incurably bad attitude and that is what this chapter intends.

Leave aside the school punishment known as Lines and there is not really an activity which you might call *writing sentences.* You write sentences in the course of doing something else - writing a letter, an essay, a novel - and in the course of doing those things, the sentences you deploy may well come in for some pretty rough handling as things get crossed out, re-arranged and so on. Such revision is often repeated and continues until the sentence does more or less what you want it to do, which is to express a thought - more generally, a *content* - but, in any case, something which is created in specific contexts of time and space and of genre. Subjected to such treatment, if sentences could scream they would. And they would scream even louder if they knew that sometimes they are being tortured for no higher purpose than to improve the style.

Some people punctuate as they go along, some return later to prick and prod at their sentences, a few decide to Pass on the task – a choice which has been the making of more than one literary reputation. But if you do it, punctuating is, by and large, a sort of underlining of what your sentence is supposed to be doing. It's meant to work towards the blissful outcome where your reader actually gets the thought you are trying to express – even if that content is ambiguous or merely suggestive.

As with old-fashioned pen and ink underlining, we can overdose and some punctuation marks seem inherently toxic, most obviously the exclamation mark which invites us to exclaim that the sentence which it follows was an exclamation. If you are not confident that you have made yourself clear or doubt the intelligence of your reader, then you double up with this crude mark and problem solved. There is an interesting history there, especially in relation to those bits of written language which now come with exclamation marks already attached. *Doh!*

As I understand them, writers of punctuation guides are people who tell us to act sensibly, do as we are told, because otherwise we will not be understood or, worse, will be dreadfully misunderstood and, not to put too fine a point on it, *Doomed.* If we don't use our Oxford Commas, we will end up (according to the Internet forums) dedicating our debut novel to:

My parents, Mother Theresa and the Pope.

That is enough to put the wind up anyone and so we dutifully prick our sentences with Oxford Commas in the same spirit as we eat our five-a-day. But we know that the medical profession does not always agree with itself and so, should we continue to a different forum, we are likely to confront damning evidence against such OC dutiful behaviour:

They gave us tea, bread, fish, and chips.

It's all wrong. Punctuating is something you do in the context of writing things and those things are so enormously contextualised, even when the prose is formal, that it is implausible to suppose that a guide book will get it right for us every time or even most of the time.

I hope that you would be at least a little shocked to discover that a letter of condolence was cut and pasted from a Condolence Letter template (198,000 results headed by www.obituarieshelp.org). You do it yourself for a letter of condolence. It's part of what makes the thing sincere. And when you are writing other things, the undergraduate essay nowadays excepted, you will often be making an effort to do it yourself and it seems a bit of a shame to give up when it comes to punctuating and sub-contract that to a guidebook. Indeed, it's more than that. You may undermine what you have been trying to express if you don't continue yourself into the punctuation. Only you can know how your sentence sounds or weighs in your mind. A rule book doesn't have a clue about that, only about how to keep the semi-colon in business. That's because rule books assume we are writing sentences with no context, no larger purpose. But they are wrong and even in the printed written word, what we write is still like an utterance to the extent that it is always situated and never an abstraction.

The relation between sentence and punctuation is rather like that which obtains between syntax and style. You can write a grammatical sentence, a sentence which is well-formed syntactically, but still reject it because it weighs in as clunky, sounds awkward, simply doesn't please. So you fiddle around to get the same result by slightly different means. At this point, it's true that in some sense you will be consulting a mental grammar book, looking for syntactic alternatives, but the test you are now applying to them is not grammatical but stylistic, and the test may be very idiosyncratic. *Style is the person themself*, as the saying goes.

Punctuation, like style, is an aspect of language use – of language pragmatics rather than syntax or semantics. But in this case there is no underlying set of syntax-like options from among which we select. Punctuation rules have been made up using conscious reasoning to rationalise and impose choices, some of them a bit odd. In the broadest sense of the term they have an ideological character, confusing helpful rules of thumb with implacable moral laws.

The most powerful evidence for the view I am advancing is to be found in the inconclusiveness of the OCD forum debates and in the fact that, at the top end of writing, there is the war against school rules which authors wage in order to defend their sentences against copy editors who are paid to see only forms, not to hear what the writer is trying to express.

6

Apostrophe's

WHY do native speakers have so much difficulty with apostrophes when writing in English? They clearly do and you can write a newspaper column shocked by the fact, the usual suspect clichés queueing to lend a hand. But the Decline of Civilization is not the only story in town.

Another story is this. The rules which govern the use of apostrophes in written English are - for some currently unknown reason - *unadapted to being learnt*. The List of Rules is quite short and believers in the List reckon that, really, the List is both easy to learn and apply. Maybe this is untrue.

There are party tricks and psychological experiments, now turned into online clickbait, which consist in giving someone a list of simple numbers to add up in their head. For certain combinations of numbers, the victim (= the experimental subject) will almost always add up wrong and arrive at a number which the joker (= the experimenter) can predict in advance. The tricks are curious because the numbers are not difficult numbers and the mistakes made are always the same. It just seems that some particular combinations of numbers touch a fault or trigger a glitch in the way we normally do addition. Many people who add up the following sequence will arrive at the same wrong answer: 1000 + 40 + 1000 + 30 + 1000 + 20 + 1000 + 10. There are similar tricks which reveal things like our difficulty in repeating things backwards or repeating them normally but at the same time inserting arbitrary words or numbers into the strings with which we have started. The numbers I just gave you do not add up to 5000. Such quirky facts point towards the idea (the theory) that some things come more *naturally* to us than others and that some things are more *learnable* than others. Tonal music comes easily to humans; atonal music doesn't. See if you can hum it while I play it.

Sometimes what linguists call *prescriptive grammar* is meant to be difficult. The idea really is to trip people up or to trip up people. In this way, prescriptivists create or reinforce a distinction between *insiders*, who have studied this particular glass bead game intensively, and *outsiders* who have not. Both spoken and written language are targets for those seeking to create social distinctions, turning language into *Language for Our Sakes*.

I remember being told by a privately-educated woman that at her girls-only school they were taught the sentence *I've got a lot of nice things*. This was a mnemonic for all the expressions which well-spoken girls were supposed to avoid:

I've should always be *I have*
and
I've got should always be *I have*
and
a lot should be *many*
and
nice should never be *nice* but instead *delightful, pleasant, fine, fun* but probably not *cute*
and
things could be *possessions* but really should be more specific and not generic (which is what *things* is).

And so a girl who opened a conversation with *I have many delightful possessions* would immediately make clear where she was coming from. The Home Counties. She had been educated into a language rule which, like the ones which Jane Fallon learnt in the preceding chapter, was aimed mainly at girls. But in this case, she had learnt by means of a terrific mnemonic device – terrific because its simple sequential structure allows you to map straight from the mnemonic onto speech. No one ever forgot this mnemonic. This bears on apostrophe rules where there is no simple mnemonic, gendered or otherwise. My guess is that the rules are more or less unlearnable and for the following reasons:

They include rules relating to demonstrating possession (*John's book*) alongside rules which relate to abbreviation or elision in speech (*John's booking the tickets*). It is more than unfortunate that the same written tic is used for these two rather different purposes, making it more difficult to deploy the tic correctly, since two different kinds of case have constantly to be canvassed: compare *John's booking the tickets* with *John's booking the tickets proved a disaster.*

The rules get mixed up with rules for plural formation: Is *The Diary of Mrs Jones* to be rendered as *Mrs Jones' Diary* or as *Mrs Jones's Diary?* Do you *Keep up with the Jones's, Keep Up With the Joness', Keep Up with the Joneses', Keep Up with the Jones? Keep up with the Joneses?....*

So the Apostrophe Rules actually operates over a complicated matrix of possibilities:

Possession + Singular
Elision + Singular
Possession + Plural
Elision + Plural

Running all the necessary tests together clearly causes us a problem. As a result, I suggest that apostrophe rules are best regarded as something for Party Tricks. In everyday life we could easily choose to omit apostrophes or avoid them and leave the Joneses of this world to keep up with themselves. The only serious alternative is to reform the all-purpose apostrophe tic and replace it with different tics, relating separately to possession and elision, singular and plural.

7

Lost in Translation

MORE than fifty years ago, my school history textbook for the French Revolution described a king called *Lewis XIV*. Even then, I thought this strange. Why translate *Louis XIV* into *Lewis XIV*? You lost information - since you now didn't know what the French actually called their king - and it wasn't necessary to do so: *Louis* is a perfectly good name in English, pronounced not so differently to the French version. I can only think that the author of this old textbook was a Scotsman – in Scotland, *Lewis* is almost certainly more common than *Louis* and I guess is a rendering of it. There is a bit of history there I am sure.

But the author of my textbook was only doing something we do all the time. In English, the Maid of Orleans is always called *Joan of Arc* and never *Jean d'Arc* or *Jean of Arc*. The translation into *Joan* may once have been a response to the fact that French *Jean* does not tell you a person's sex, though nowadays we don't feel the need to convert *Jean Genet* to *John Genet*. There are other things which are never translated: *l'Arc de Triomphe* is never called *the Triumph Arch* or *the Triumphal Arch* but usually *the Arc de Triomphe*. And *the Champs-Élysées* is never - but never - *the Elysian Fields*. You may not have realised that they are.

If I was writing a handbook for translation, I would start it with one rule: *Avoid translations which lose information unnecessarily.* Many English versions of capital city names fail to meet this simple requirement. Consider three examples.

Roma is rendered *Rome* in English, so we lose a bit of information about what the Romans do in Roma, namely, how they pronounce the name of their capital. There appears to be no reason why *Roma* should not be rendered *Roma* in English. If we can take a holiday in Verona, why not one in Roma?

Wien becomes *Vienna*, a nicer name it's true but desperately misleading. It's maybe helpful that the "W" becomes "V" to reflect differences in how these letters are pronounced in German and English, though in reality it's only done for *Wien*. As a rule, German-language place names are usually left unaltered: think *Wannsee, Weimar, Wiesbaden, Worms, Wuppertal.* Back to Vienna and why isn't *Wien* either retained or rendered as *Vien*? What is that " - na" doing on the end? It looks and sounds like pure invention.

København becomes wonderful, wonderful *Copenhagen*. This is massively defective. First, there is no need to change the "K" to a "C" to indicate the pronunciation – kicking "K" works no different to curly "C" in English. Second, it's true that when accents (diacritical marks) are missing from our keyboards we need a substitution rule, but in this case the correct substitution for "ø" is "oe" which gets closer to the Danish pronunciation than the completely incorrect "o" which in English leads to the bad pronunciation *Co-penhagen*. Third, when *-havn* becomes *-hagen* we lose the information that this city is a port, a harbour, a haven. But there are many English harbour names which have the ending *-haven* (*Newhaven,*

Peacehaven, Whitehaven ...) and only the very dim-witted would fail to pick up the link between -*havn* and -*haven*. In addition (and fourth), -*hagen* removes information which might help us to the correct pronunciation: it takes away a soft "a" and gives us a hard "a". Fifth, we have this slippage from "b" to "p" which is unnecessary even though there is a complicated issue about "b" and "p" pronunciation. In short, *Copenhagen* is a disaster. In English, the Danish capital could more helpfully be referred to as *Koebenhavn* or *K'benhavn* or better still, if I have persuaded you to come onside, *K'b'nhavn*.

I could go on at great length. What we are looking at are fossilised bits of written language which either had no rationale to begin with or have since lost it. Since we have managed to turn *Peking* into *Beijing, Bombay* into *Mumbai*, and *Calcutta* into *Kolkata,* it doesn't seem unreasonable to pay some attention to what nearer neighbours call their cities. Of course, as in other cases, it helps to start off by not feeling quite so hostile to them.

8

Ungrammarly

DRIVE along an English road and you will soon see a sign giving you *Advanced Warning* of forthcoming road-works. We do a lot of roadworks. Like everyone else, I try hard not to be a pedant but I do smile. When you give warning in advance that something is going to happen, you give an *Advance Warning*. Part of the explanation of the error must lie in sound similarity: say *Advance warning* quickly enough and it sounds more or less the same as *Advanced warning*. But this coincidence does not explain why the makers of road signs have picked *Advanced* rather than the grammatically correct *Advance* for their signs. True, the sounds are more or less the same, but why pick the wrong version when it comes to spelling?

I think there must be a chain of association to other uses of *Advanced*. For example, in England, school students used to take exams called *Ordinary Levels* when they were about sixteen and more difficult - more advanced - exams when they were eighteen. The Ordinary Levels now have new names, but the latter exams are still called Advanced Levels. These are not Levels *in advance of* something, but Levels which are *more advanced than something else*, namely the old Ordinary Levels.

By analogy, an Advanced Warning would be a warning more advanced than some other kind of warning – for example, an Advance Warning. That is not the kind of warning road sign makers are giving you. But they have very often seen the words *Advanced Level* in print – they are a regular newspaper topic and, in addition, sign makers' children may well bring home bits of paper about Advanced Level courses. The sign makers then just go with the flow of words they have read in quite other contexts.

I suspect that in time *Advanced warning* will take over from the grammatically correct *Advance warning* just as we now *refute* instead of *reject*. Here, for example, is the 11th March 2014 front page of the *Financial Times* – normally a good pedant about these things:

> *...the wealthy would find ways around the proposed tax grab, especially now they have had so much advanced warning ...*

I suppose that is one of the problems when you are of advanced years – you see these things coming in advance.

*

I was failing old writing to the wastebin and came across a poem which begins:

> *And to whom should I tell my stories*
> *If not to you?*

It continued and it has gone to the wastebin, its fate sealed by the would-be poetic *And* followed promptly by the punctiliousness of *to whom*. Why didn't I just write:

> *Who should I tell my stories to*
> *If not to you?*

After all, this was supposed to be a lyric poem. Who

wants a pedant as a lover? I had forgotten about the poem
which goes back (let's exaggerate a bit) thirty years, but
without knowing it, I somehow learnt my lesson. In a
much more recent piece of work, I closed an essay titled
"Letters Not About Love" with a three-sentence coda:

> *Who am I to write my letters to, if not to you?*
> *The weather here is nice today.*
> *I could reserve our old table.*

Ungrammarly and better. The problem with the grammatical *to whom* construction in English is that it is now -
whatever the history - marked as a scrupulous choice,
one of those things you can use for virtue signalling. The
grammatically incorrect *who ... to* construction is rela-
tively unmarked. It is what comes spontaneously to most
people when they haven't got a grammarian on their back.
Of course, if the object of your desire is a grammarist
then you might be advised to choose *to whom* for your
lyric, but otherwise not.

I have argued in chapter 6 that punctuation can't really
be understood in terms of Rules but is all about contextual
appropriateness. Now I want to say the same about at
least some aspects of syntax. The moment a syntactic
feature loses a solid presence in the living language and
keeps a hold only in the minds of specialists and obsessives, it becomes something which a writer uses at their
peril. Anywhere on the grammar front where indignant
forum posts are fighting a rear-guard action to save
civilisation, you need to watch your words carefully and
avoid theirs.

9

Languages and Identity Politics

In terms of their grammars, languages do not form a continuum. There are structural discontinuities which mean that when you learn a foreign language, usually you have to learn much more than a new vocabulary. Sometimes the structures are radically different; Finnish is not a bit like the other Scandinavian languages. In fact, from a structural point of view, it is most like Hungarian. So in language typologies, these two monstrously difficult languages are grouped together as Finno-Ugric.

The other main Scandinavian languages (Danish, Norwegian, Swedish) are more different now than they once were. There is still a high level of mutual intelligibility – a Swedish speaker can understand a Danish speaker, even though they cannot speak Danish, and the Danish speaker can understand the Swedish speaker. But as part of nation-building efforts, the three languages were developed away from their common core. This has both advantages and disadvantages. On the plus side, standardisation - achieved through control over what is taught in schools and then through such things as editorial policies in publishing houses - does result in more efficient communication. It takes less time to understand what someone else is saying, or make sense of what someone else has written, the closer they are to you in terms of syntax, phonology, vocabulary and spelling. And there is less chance of misunderstanding.

The disadvantage is that as you move a language away

from its core or away from another language, you eventually reach a point where you can't understand your near neighbours and they can't understand you. To communicate, at least one of you has to learn what has now become a foreign language.

Nation-building and nationalism more generally do have positive features. If you think of yourself as Czech and are proud of that fact, then that provides quite a good basis for simple forms of civic consciousness. You're Czech and proud of it and that's one reason you don't drop litter in the street. But nationalisms, like all forms of identity politics, often lead to excesses of one kind or another. Some are distinctly unpleasant. Others are more simply tiresome. Language policies are often in the latter category.

Everyone knows that the French, who maintain a very strong sense of national identity, have an absurd relation to their language. They don't want it to change. They don't want Foreign Words contaminating their language. So they want you to say *site-web* and not *website* because it's more French (just like *Pages Jaunes* for *Yellow Pages*). But to demand that a language does not change is an impossible demand, a King Canute kind of demand. The French don't want a foreigner-contaminated language but whether they like it or not, that's what they have always had to live with. It goes with being an imperial power.

Nor do Russians and Ukrainians want languages with open borders. They insist on quite minor differences between their languages when, from the point of view of communication, it would be very useful to go with the flow of language mixing and what linguists call Free Variation – which means, roughly, that one form is reckoned as good as another; think of *Hallo* and *Hello* in both spoken and written English. After all, these Slavic language speakers do share a long common border and most of them, left to their own devices, would be happy to go with the flow whichever side of the border they happen to be on.

Rather than tolerate Free Variation, however, the authorities - political and cultural - are very insistent on staking their claims to difference. In Cyrillic, the spelling is the same, but the town which Russians would call *Gomel* has to be transliterated as *Homel* if you don't want to annoy your Ukrainian friends. Likewise, for Russians it's *Sevastopol* but for Ukrainians it's *Sevastopil.* The sensible thing might be to accept free variation, as one does for *Hallo / Hello*.

Making an issue of *Sevastopol / Sevastopil* adds yet another layer to multiple and more serious problems, and helps harden differences which would be better blurred. At worst, it falls into the same kind of sectarianism which, for example, separates the Russian Orthodox Church from Old Believers, themselves then divided against each other by multiple minor differences. In Crimea, there is the additional fact that the original Tatar population called towns by quite different names which had official recognition until the mass deportations of 1944, from which the Tatars have never recovered.

Languages with open borders mean that more people can join in a game – business, sport, pleasure, tourism – whereas linguistic identitarianism is designed to exclude. Where absolute precision is required, then it's often necessary to use a special language which might be Latin (think of the development of theology or medicine) or nowadays is more likely to be English (air traffic control). It's always a good question to ask of any policy *What are we trying to achieve?* And if the answer is *We are turning our backs on those awful people next door* then it's probably a bad policy.

Part Two

10

Writing: The Teachable and Unteachable in Creative Writing

In autumn 1997, the University of Sussex introduced a Creative Writing strand into its long-running MA pro-gramme Language, the Arts and Education *on which I had taught since its inception in the early 1980s. In July 1997, I was installed at the Centre Culturel International de Cérisy-la-Salle for a conference* L'animal autobio-graphique *devoted to Jacques Derrida's work and with his participation. While I was there, I wrote the following as part of my self-preparation for teaching on the new MA strand. I call it an essay but it reads as a fairly formal lecture. It has been edited for this book.*

*

THE title of this chapter is expansive enough, but it already excludes all that is contrasted with writing as speech. Writing and speech are different, though con-temporary reports of their difference have been exag-gerated, in ways to which this essay may contribute a corrective. If speech is excluded from my proposed subject matter, so too is literacy, as a mental and social fact and problem. I shall not be concerned with the acquisition of the skill of writing, nor the social man-agement of its distribution. Writing has many genres and we who are literate write letters, shopping lists, school essays, poems, novels, and so on – but already enough to mobilize the superordinate genres of non-literary and literary writing. And for the rest of this essay, *writing* will mean literary writing.

So what is literary writing? One influential contemporary approach (that of Roland Barthes and many others) has it that literary writing is intransitive, unlike the non-literary which is transitive, oriented toward the standard aims of communication. Writing is intransitive when it is writing just for the sake of writing and when what matters, to author and to reader alike, is the character - the quality - of the very writing itself.

But what could qualify as such a quality other than the style of the writing? Is not literary writing style itself? *L'écriture, c'est le style même.* Unfortunately for the gesture toward La Rochefoucauld, it is impossible to sustain any unified notion of style for it immediately breaks apart into at least three aspects that it is as well to set down here and now.

First, there are formal styles or registers that have a conventional existence and already prescribe how some piece of literary writing is to be executed. What makes something a haiku or a limerick is not up to the individual writer. The forms already exist and are to hand, ready to be re-used.

Second, there is that aspect of a writer's style which is not deliberately crafted but which exists as symptomatic or indexical of a concrete individual's mannerisms and can be used to determine authorship. If you discover a piece of writing that may be by Shakespeare, you don't determine this question by literary judgment alone, or at all. If the piece is sufficiently extended in length, you run it through a computer program that will tell you whether the style is Shakespeare's. A perfectly analogous approach in art history, originated by Giovanni Morelli, consists in determining authenticity by looking at how minor details such as ear lobes are painted. The assumption is that these are parts of the painting on which the painter would have worked in a more relaxed and less attentive manner, thus leaving behind a symptomatic signature.

Third, there is crafted style to which the (serious) writer is supposed to devote his or her best efforts and in terms of which literary identity is at least partly (and maybe more than partly) established.

If we turn our attention to educational programmes devoted to the teaching of creative writing, it is easy and convenient to suppose that what has to be done is familiarize the student with the registers of literary writing and help him or her with the crafting of a personal style. And this is part of the truth. But not the whole truth, because it is not the whole truth that literary writing is the style itself. For at least in relation to prose genres (to which I shall now confine my attention), writing is about the making of imagined worlds, in which states of affairs, characters, and events are represented and - I want to say - *represented with feeling*. For this phrase *represented with feeling* I shall now substitute the word *expressed*, and say that in prose writing imagined worlds are expressed. Those worlds can be more or less fictional, more or less grounded in fact or personal experience. They can be very small or astonishingly large.

This is not to collapse imaginative writing into communication, but it is to say that such writing is larger than its stylistic aspect, even though what is expressed in writing is probably inseparable from (is organic with) how it is expressed. This recognition will, among other things, promptly upset any idea that teaching creative writing is about teaching a kind of craft skill. For now "becoming a writer" changes into something more than being able to turn words adeptly, as a wordsmith. "Becoming a writer" will also involve accessing or inventing mental worlds and representing them with feeling. Nor is this to be achieved in any mechanical, before-and-after sense that the representation is subsequent to the world's being identified, but rather in the sense that the worlds accessed are always-already represented with feeling, though their final realization on the page may require considerable crafting. Becoming a writer involves being or becoming *imaginative* in a particular way: being able to imagine worlds peopled with characters, enlivened by events, and furnished with more or less elaborate settings. It is far from obvious that being imaginative is something teachable, nor is it obvious what constitutes a learning environment in which the imagination will flourish.

One way to get some purchase on the question, *Can imagination be taught or nurtured?* is to consider what might be the obstacles to anyone's being or becoming imaginative. I identify two main categories of obstacle.

First, as a mental activity, exercise of the imagination may be curtailed by limitations of general or specific intelligence. For purposes of this essay, I need take no view on how significant this is.

Second, unless you believe that the mind (mental activity) is always and everywhere transparent to itself, that all its operations are reflexively available to itself, and that all our mental activity can be co-ordinated in a co-operative endeavour to achieve our conscious goals – unless you believe all this, then you have to allow that there is room for imaginative activity to fail in what it seeks to achieve. The theory of the unconscious mind, as it has been developed since Freud, is a way of showing how the exercise of imagination may be limited by the operation of unconscious *transfers* and *resistances* that distort or block the free flow of imaginative engagement.

As a preliminary sketch, my thinking goes something like this: a writer trying (consciously) to represent a world of people and events can be disrupted in that practice by interference from unconscious mental material that has been activated in and by the writing. For example, emerging characters in a story may get transferred onto them emotions originally attaching to other (real) characters – paradigmatically, one's mother or father. This unconscious process is not (by definition) available to the writer for conscious monitoring and reflection in the form of the question, *Is what is now happening good for the story I'm trying to write?* Consequently, there is at the most banal level some chance that the transfer will be bad for the story, tending to derail it, rather than strengthen it and make it resonate.

Likewise, an emerging story, if consciously reflected upon, may require representations of people or events which because of the operation of unconscious resistance cannot be accessed by the writer. So the representations go missing and the story suffers. It would, for example, be a gross mistake to suppose that all you need for the writing of a good sex scene in a novel is the right craft skill, learnt in the eighth week of term. The scene, even when consciously and conscientiously embarked upon, may be sabotaged by the operation of unconscious resistance and that is an individual problem and not really a topic for a seminar.

In the same way, anxieties about political correctness can inhibit both writer and reader. The writer fails to let rip and really give us a character who breaks the rules, the reader tries to keep a straight face and not laugh at something which is very funny. Both end up behaving like they are overseen by a severe Sunday School teacher. The 1997 novel *Europa* by Tim Parks is a wonderfully written and very funny story of people behaving very incorrectly, but has never had the recognition it deserves because it is discomforting for readers trying too hard to be virtuous.

It begins to look as if the practice of writing will go better, will encounter fewer obstacles, to the extent that we have achieved some kind of self-possession, some kind of self-knowledge. This is not something that creative writing courses are there to teach. Nor could they teach it, for self-knowledge comes about through experience, through the unforeseen challenges of life, and more specifically through the challenges encountered in close relationships and sometimes in counselling, psychotherapy, and psychoanalysis.

I want to flesh out this sketch by looking more closely at the idea of unconscious transfer(ence) and illustrating some of its varieties. In a one-to-one therapeutic situation, a patient may seek (desire) the therapist's approval or love, and this may result in the foregrounding of psychic material that is thought likely to elicit such responses and in the withholding of other material. The patient, just like any good politician, can be economical with the truth. A writer can also seek (desire) approval or love from an (unknown) audience, and this desire can be transferred into the writing being done, so that the writing is run through with the desire for approval.

Equally, a patient may transferentially fear an analyst's disapproval, or loss of interest, or anger and may seek to circumvent and prevent their occurrence. In parallel, a writer may write anticipating a certain reaction from the (unknown) audience and seek to contain or displace it. As a scientific writer, Freud does this all the time, constantly trying to disarm by anticipation the negative reactions to his work that he expects.

Related to this is the situation in which a patient, anticipating an analyst's hate, may seek to take control of the situation by appropriating the anticipated hate and expressing it as self-hate. A writer can do the same.

As a final example, consider that a patient may assume in the analyst the same desires as their own and may therefore approach the analyst collusively, expecting agreement as to the desirable. A writer may do the same thing. The obvious example is provided by academic writing where "we" is often written as expressive of an expectation of agreement. There is also collusive writing in literature – something easily spotted when the text dates from a past century.

But why are such transfers (necessarily) bad things? Let me try to answer this by taking the example of self-hate and drawing a distinction. There is nothing wrong in trying to envision a fictional world in which the characters express self-hate. But the writing will fail, I want to argue, in proportion to any inability in the writer to bring their own self-hate under some kind of conscious, reflexive awareness. In the absence of such awareness, real self-hatred will continue to express itself transferentially (symptomatically) across and through the literary text, rather than expressively or symbolically within the worked text. And the literary text is not supposed to be a symptom, though the goal of keeping it symptom-free will never be completely achieved. Writers are human beings, not disembodied minds. They can strive but they will always at some point fail.

In Jane Austen's *Persuasion* there is an awful chapter IX in volume II where Mrs Smith, more or less invented for the purpose, is allowed a very long monologue (pages of it!) to trash the character of Mr William Elliot and knock him out of any possible contention, leaving the way clear for the return of the gallant Captain Wentworth. It feels like the author has some kind of personal grudge; there is something unbalanced about that chapter IX which makes this reader feel that the text at this point is a symptom rather than a symbol necessary for the development of the plot.

I can come at what I am trying to say by another direction and suggest that the commonplace of a writer *finding a voice* can be given at least part of its meaning in terms of the overcoming of transfers and resistances, and by a roundabout route, that is the claim I want now to try to sustain. The idea of a writer finding a voice requires careful scrutiny. After all, it appears to transgress the rule or ruling that speech and writing are separate orders of reality. The claim I want to advance is that finding a voice is important in just the same way as speaking sincerely, authentically and for oneself, is important in everyday life. Not to speak with a full word is always to speak with the voice of others or another – society, party, church, mother or father. This idea of the *full word* I take from Jacques Lacan's early work and is the subject of the next chapter.

To speak with a full word does not always involve speaking in new words, but may require only that one accents the words of another as fully, authentically one's own. By way of example only, consider that within versions of Protestantism like Scots Presbyterianism, *doubt* plays a constructive role, since it enables one (God willing) to come to a faith that is based in personal conviction rather than family or communal inheritance. The crisis of doubt functions to move one from dependence to independence. One's words may not change, but the way they are spoken changes fundamentally. In chapter 1 of this book, I have already made use of the same idea.

It cannot be quite the same with writing, since as readers we reckon to be able to locate where writers find their voice in what they write. In other words, when a writer finds a voice something lisible changes. It remains to characterize what, and this I shall shortly attempt.

But there is an assumption here that a voice is always something that is found, in time. A writer never starts with a full-fledged voice of his or her own, any more than a painter starts with a style or a philosopher with a vision. They all begin in dependence, by which I mean "under the influence" of what their schools have taught them and of what they have read and seen.

Awareness that one is "under the influence" may be followed by an attempt (a neurotic attempt) to shorten the lengthy passage toward finding a voice by means of a conscious but premature rejection of the influences to which one has been subject. Adolescent *rebellion* is a lot like that. Alternatively, there can be recognition of subjection combined with its full and conscious acceptance which, when it takes a slavish form, yields what is often called *academicism*. Failure to recognize dependence means that we go on blithely producing while always in dependence. This is what *traditionalism* is about.

Negatively, finding a voice means avoiding the traps of rebelliousness, academicism, and traditionalism. Positively, I think it is relevant that the judgment that a writer has found his or her voice is made by an audience, so that a voice becomes a matter of *recognition* (like the style of a painter). But what is being recognized? I want to say that it is something like *the full imaginative expression of a bounded individuality.* In this statement the word *bounded* plays a crucial role.

I can sketch this crucial role by going back to the side of the writer and imagining that finding a voice is a bit like finding a key in music. In a science fiction scenario, one can imagine all possible texts being run past a writer who selects those they could have written. In such a scenario, the voice you have found provides the principle of selection; it picks out texts in which particular kinds of world have been represented with a particular feeling tone and in a characteristic manner (style). If you are Samuel Beckett or Virginia Woolf, you can confidently select from among the texts run past you the Samuel Beckett-texts and the Virginia Woolf-texts. If you haven't (found) a voice, then the texts you select will come with a variety of signatures, perhaps not even including your own.

One day in a seminar I was attending, a student challenged Roland Barthes on something he had just said and claimed that Barthes elsewhere was telling us to be revolutionaries (*Soyez révolutionnaires!*). *I couldn't have said that*, replied Barthes, *it's not my style.* That was true; Barthes never told people what to do.

In an essay that has been very short of references to other works on writing, it now occurs to me that there is at least an analogy between what I am saying here and what Lucien Goldmann said many years ago in his study of Pascal and Racine, *Le Dieu Caché*, translated as *The Hidden God*. From within a broad sociological Marxism, Goldmann tries to answer the question, *What singles out the great work or writer?* His answer is that it is the work or writer that best expresses the vision of a class or group at a particular time and frees that vision from accretions that do not properly belong to it but which in our everyday worlds are always and everywhere to some extent mixed up with our own way of seeing. The great writer is a very selective filter and a very acute distinguisher. But this is to say that the great writer is strong on boundaries, on demarcating what belongs and what does not belong. I am saying that finding a voice is a lot like that.

A few paragraphs back, I also said that it had to do with overcoming transfers and resistances. I can connect this to what I have just been arguing if I say that transfers and resistances are varieties of boundary problem. So in transference we bring to an encounter with a person, or with our emerging text, images and feelings that do not belong there but have been brought in from elsewhere. Transference transgresses a boundary, a boundary necessary to keeping a personal encounter authentic at the level of I and Thou, and necessary to keeping the story as *this* story, rather than some other (perhaps lost and forgotten) one. Resistance works in a different way, preventing us from filling the space within the boundary, whether as inhibition of our contact with another person or inhibition in the expression of what properly falls within the story we have marked out.

We never lead our own lives to the full because there are transfers and resistances we never overcome. In our writing, even our best literary writing, there will also and always be the trace of that which we have not been able to efface. Life and writing have this in common, that they are always human, all too human.

11

The Empty Word
and the Full Word

Success in writing creatively is linked to the notion of "finding a voice" and this is turn is explored through psychoanalytic notions, including Jacques Lacan's idea of the "parole pleine", the full word, equivalent to Donald Winnicott's "True Self". Such ideas are relevant because we value fiction writing when it succeeds in creating imagined worlds that we find ourselves animating as expressions of significant emotion and feeling.

*

WHEN we sit down to write fictions, we may hope to discover something about ourselves on the way and may even have that as an aim – courses of study exist now in therapeutic writing. But we may not discover anything about ourselves, and may achieve no more than the writing of a fiction. In parallel, aiming only to write fiction, with no hope or aim other than that, we may nonetheless chance upon moments of self-discovery as when we suddenly remember something about our lives that we had not thought about for so long that it had become lost and forgotten. It is little different when reading an autobiographical fiction of childhood that evokes memories of our own past. If you are the right age, British, and reading Kate Atkinson's *Behind the Scenes at the Museum* the words "Andy Pandy", "Bill and Ben" and "the Coronation" are triggers to reminiscence.

Self-discovery is not something of which we can assure ourselves by careful planning and, by definition, whatever it is that is lost or unknown in ourselves cannot be known in advance of the journeys, including fictional journeys, we undertake. This means that we may be surprised by what we find and may not like it one little bit. But do we really make self-discoveries? Isn't the philosophical realism that there is something *In Here*, something inner and true, waiting to be discovered, untenable as an account of our relationship to ourselves? How can I write blithely of *self-discovery* when all around me I read that (really? essentially?) all we can reasonably hope for is *self-invention*, self-improvisation, plausible story-telling, in which the frontier between truth and fiction is not so much transgressed as abolished? I think, for example, of how these claims influence the writings of Adam Phillips in such books as *On Kissing, Tickling and Being Bored* (1993).

The binary opposition between self-discovery and self-invention is so neat that it really ought to arouse at least a little deconstructive suspicion, and the search for a third term. When I sit down to write a story it would be true to say that I make it up as I go along. But classical rhetoric presented three aspects of making it up as if they were temporally ordered. So invention (*inventio* - having ideas) precedes organisation (*dispositio* - beginnings, middles and ends) and that precedes the actual business of speaking or writing well (*elocutio* - sentence structure and phrasing). It is easy to go along with this. But then we have allowed ourselves to be taken in by a very misleading picture. A much better picture would have it that invention and organisation go on *in the elocution itself* – in the acts of speaking or writing (and analogous acts in other symbolic fields). There is no essential

temporal ordering. The rhetorical trio which trips off the
tongue so easily - *inventio, dispositio, elocutio* - is
analytic, not a classification of an essential order of real
time events. It is not a bit like *Veni, Vidi, Vici - I came,
I saw, I conquered* - which has to be done in that order.
Only in the elocution, *the enactment*, do the ideas and
organisation become embodied, and disembodied they
are of limited interest. Nobody offers creative writing
courses in the writing of synopses. From the other side,
this is also to say that there is not only enactment
(*elocutio*). Invention and disposition are also lisible in
the enactment.

I'm going to pin my hopes on *enactment* as a possible
middle term which may help avert a rather silly war
between the advocates of self-discovery and the advocates of self-invention. It may allow us to see that
self-discovery is not (essentially) about introspection, and
that what is often called self-invention is (actually) self-
enactment. For enactment to do the job I want, I also have
to draw a distinction between something which I shall
call, following Jacques Lacan, the *Empty Word* and
something which in contrast is the *Full Word*.

If we are unhealthy, we may act out unresolved
psychological conflicts in our behaviour. Acting out is
something to which we are *liable*, rather than something
of which we are *capable* – to use a distinction I owe to
the work of Rom Harré (Harré and Madden 1975). It can
happen to us anywhere: in the living room, the bedroom,
the seminar room, the consulting room. I think that we
can also act out in our writing, often in obscure ways.
Acting out is both full and empty. It is indeed filled up
with something coming from inside us (from our mental
life), but it is empty in that in it we lose ourselves as
agents, as responsible beings, as individuals capable of

reflexively monitored action, to put it in the language of Anthony Giddens (1979). So we are blind to what we are doing and to who we are.

There are desperate measures which individuals can take to bring acting out under (apparent) reflexive control, so that it at least begins to look like something they are doing rather than something which is happening to them. We call these desperate measures by such names as rationalisation, self-deception, projection, and denial. Just as the acting out is full of us, so these measures are empty of us: the very meaning of rationalisation is that it is the giving of a reason which is a pseudo-reason, a false reason, an empty reason. Characteristically, when we rationalise we draw on the socially available stock of acceptable excuses for bad behaviour. In other words, we seek outside for ways to make ourselves acceptable to ourselves and to others. Lost in the original acting out we lose ourselves again in the rationalisation by means of which we try to recuperate ourselves to ourselves and re-integrate ourselves with others.

We move away from acting out and rationalisation to the extent that we can begin to express what we feel, say what we mean, and mean what we say. We may need some kind of psychotherapy to help us achieve that, and so we can characterise the object of psychotherapy as helping us towards a full word, an enactment of self which does not leave us split from our feelings, including our oldest and most difficult feelings.

What has all this got to do with writing? There is a craft task in writing which can be discharged more or less well, producing a more or less well-crafted story. We can award marks, if we need to, for invention, disposition and elocution. Good marks mean that we are satisfied that the work is well formed. But at another level, we may be dissatisfied with a piece of work which stylistically is "all right." And we may find ourselves having recourse to that metaphor which transgresses the boundary between speech and writing, and asking whether the writer has (yet) "found their voice." My central claim is that the distinction between writing which lacks some important factor X and writing with a found voice can be connected to the distinction between the empty word and the full word.

Finding a voice is something which can only be achieved and confirmed in enactment; you don't find your voice by silently soliloquising. You find your voice by doing something with your voice. For a writer, finding a voice is about writing with feeling. It is about achieving a sureness of touch which allows a reader to animate the bare text with a feeling tone and to go on reading with a sense that the author-in-the-text is not going to go out of their emotional depth, even though they may lead us into waters which we find difficult and murky. A writer is also a guide. Together we are searching for lost and unrecognised experience, and for human beings experience is always felt experience. We don't just see the sunrise, we are elated by it; we don't just watch the sea raging, we are awed by it.

But this invocation of such sublime feelings as elation and awe probably begs a question. Why shouldn't we be looking for fictions of experience which are more inventive than I am now suggesting, fictions which surf the phenomenal rather than plumb the depths? The phenomenal is part of our experience, and close observation of it part of the talent and training of the writer as well as the painter. But the Impressionists - to take an obvious example - are more than painters of the surface play of light on light reflective surfaces. They are painters of mood and vision, and their paintings are consequently animated with a feeling tone. If they were not, they would be that much the less interesting. So it is with writers. Writers do actually have to observe: Vladimir Nabokov wrote his road-novel *Lolita* on the back of being driven thousands of miles across America, sitting in the back seat writing notes. Those road trips are themselves the subject of an interesting book by Richard Roper (2015). But, of course, not everyone is a Nabokov who can turn detail into something more than detail, imparting mood or extracting feeling. When people post reviews on sites like www.goodreads.com then they will quite often acknowledge the detail or the history in a novel but then express their disappointment using words like *flat* or *lifeless*. But it's not that the individual words lack some *afflatus*, as if the writer has not blown into them hard enough. It's a problem with how the prose is structured, how the words are arranged, and getting that right is all about having a feeling for what you are trying to express.

Roland Barthes seems, at least in some of his work, to miss this difference between the detail and the delivery; he sees the importance of the fact-gathering and ignores the uncertainty of its animation. So in his famous essay "Death of the Author," he characterises the writer as really a *scriptor* – someone who "no longer bears with him passions, humours, feelings, impressions," but rather is possessed of an "immense dictionary from which he draws a writing that can know no halt."

Inadvertently, I have in the preceding paragraphs twice used the idea of something animated with a feeling tone. This idea comes to me from the work of Peter Kivy and Richard Wollheim. They say that an unlearnt ability (or liability) of human beings is their capacity to see one thing in another. At one level, this is the capacity or liability to see the face in the fire, the giant in the clouds. At another level, it is the capacity or liability to see a landscape as melancholy, a pansy as thoughtful. We are also able and liable to see such qualities in a work of art, not least when they are expressed there. So the music strikes us as sad or lively, the painting as gloomy, the novel as anguished. But when we animate in this way, we do it (I want to say, and I am wondering if I can get beyond the standard metaphor) from inside ourselves, whether as makers of the art work or as audience for it. We reach into that vast reservoir which is our experience and our ways of responding to experience, connecting it and framing it. In this optic, Roland Barthes' characterisation of the writer as *scriptor* looks less plausible in relation to basic ways of experiencing the world: either we have those ways available to us, or at least analogues of those ways, or we are at a loss. If we have never experienced depression (let us say), either in ourselves or in another, I find it hard to see how from books or conversations we could do much more than mimic it in an artistic work, rather than express it fully and that means that while an audience might catch our drift, they would not get to the point of unwilled animation of the work with its appropriate feeling tone. And to that extent, they would remain unsatisfied. This critical thought could be connected to the extensive discussion in philosophical aesthetics of the concept of the "perfect forgery". For if we need only the talent of a *scriptor*, then in literature the perfect forgery can indeed be constructed. In his own literary work, Barthes most certainly draws on a deep reservoir of his own feelings. That is perhaps most obvious in his short book on photography *Camera Lucida* where he is mourning the death of his mother.

Where experience has been subject to repression, we

are denied reflexive access to it: that's what the word implies. We can act out in ways driven by the continuing psychic efficacy of repressed material, but we cannot enact it. So the repression blocks us either creatively as writers or imaginatively as readers. The experience of trying to write, like that of trying to talk in psychoanalysis, can return repressed material to consciousness. It then has to be dealt with by the person whose repressed material it is, if it is to be shaped into writing. But just as I wanted to deny that the trio of invention, disposition and elocution represented a necessary chronological ordering, so I want to suggest that it may be that repressed material which comes to the surface in the course of writing may be dealt with (worked through) in the writing itself. The working through does not have to be anterior to or exterior to the writing. This is to imply that at some points what we distinguish as the psychologically individual author or writer, on the one hand, and the implied textual author or imagined fictive narrator, on the other, may be operating simultaneously and in the same words. We then have two faces to the same text. It is an occupational hazard of literary criticism to see now one face, now the other, even in the same sentence.

The line of thinking developed in the preceding paragraphs is intended not so much to contradict "Death of the Author" theorising which in the past fifty years or more has insisted on the autonomy of the literary text in relation to its psychologically real author, but rather to make this simple point: that literary texts are double faced. On the one face, they are indeed works of art which have left behind their real creators: *writing is the destruction of every voice, of every point of origin,* says Barthes. As such, writing possesses expressive qualities and internal properties (formal, relational properties) which we can value emotionally and aesthetically. But on the other face, the words of the literary text can appear as expressive of the life of the psychologically real author, and serve as evidence for the character and opinions of that author. So it is quite possible to read a literary text, now from one side, now from the other. We can Gestalt switch our mode of attention. Barthes, and the many others who have written in the same vein, could be taken as trying to show us how not to get our modes of attention mixed up. But it's hard and there is a book to be written which would argue that mixing up is inevitable. If writing is the *destruction of every voice,* why are we so keen that our novels should have a single real author rather than come out of a workshop where labour is divided?

It remains true under this view of the literary text as double faced that it is a failing in a literary work of art if it obliges us to eke out a literary reading with biographical data about the author. There is, for example, poetry which is too "private" in that its line by line meaning can only shine when we bring to bear knowledge of quite specific detail of the poet's biography. When that is the case, the poetry is rightly judged unsatisfactory.

To think as I am thinking is to be humanist about human beings and humanist about art. It is to say that human life is not (essentially) a fiction and that fictions are (essentially) about human lives. In chapter 3, I briefly considered Milan Kundera's way of stating such a claim. Where else might one find such humanism expressed in these anti-humanist times?

*

As an epigraph to his 1953 Rome Discourse, *Fonction et Champ de la Parole et du Langage en Psychanalyse* [Function and Field of Speech and Language in Psychoanalysis], Jacques Lacan inscribes this line from a prayer in *L'Internelle Consolacion*, dating from 1403:

> *Donne en ma bouche parole vraie et estable et fay de moy langue caulte*
> Give me a true and stable word in my mouth and make of me a cautious tongue (Anthony Wilden's translation).

Lacan uses this epigraph as a way of introducing a distinction between the Empty Word and the true or Full Word, and this in turn defines the aspiration of psychoanalysis to enable the emergence of Truth in the Real. Empirical reality includes the rationalisations, projections, denials and disavowals which make our words empty rather than full as expressions of a personal truth. Empirical reality is not (in Lacan's Hegelian vision) the Real, for the Real is the Rational where everything is what it ought to be. Personal Truth (Truth in the Real) is not to be thought of as the acquisition of new knowledge (for example, theoretical knowledge couched in the language of psychoanalysis), but rather as the recognition of what we already know, but only unconsciously. As Lacan puts it, in Wilden's translation, "The unconscious is that chapter of my history which is marked by a blank or occupied by a falsehood: it is the censored chapter. But the truth can be found again; it is most often already written down elsewhere" – for example, written down as neurotic symptom. Such finding or recognition is best looked upon not as something ever fully achievable - the unconscious always slips away from us - but as a rational endeavour towards something which is only achievable asymptotically, always liable to deferral and defeat.

*

What I have done in this chapter is no more than to suggest an extension and application of this kind of thinking to the processes and results of literary endeavour, making the traditional notion of "finding one's voice" an analogue of Lacan's Full Word. In turn, Lacan's Full Word plays exactly the part in his thought that the idea of the plain, old-fashioned *True Self* plays in Donald Winnicott's. Lacan's Empty Word is Winnicott's *False Self*. So the connections I am making are not just to one version of psychoanalysis, but are meant to be more general in resonance. Finding a voice just is the emergence of Truth or a True Self in the Real of writing.

In writing, one is at a sort of double jeopardy: that one may find oneself blocked expressively, unable to write a full word, and blocked critically, unable to bring critical candour to what one has succeeded in putting on paper. It is often only the former problem which receives attention; consider for a moment the latter. In writing, just as in speaking, the unconscious finds a way to express itself. Freud gives examples in *The Psychopathology of Everyday Life* though obviously we have to do with much more than slips of the pen. To be blocked critically is to be unable to integrate what we have unconsciously expressed into our conscious plan of writing. We are in the position of not being able to control our writing, which to that degree remains unmeasured. Inability to bring one's "critical faculties" (as we call them) to bear on one's writing is just as much a writing block as the primary inability to get any words onto the blank paper before one. There is a further possibility of blockage caused by hypertrophy of the critical faculties which leads to the rejection of everything one writes. Such hypertrophy is like a punitive superego, a vigilant censor committed to extinguishing every last flicker of self-expression.

In a psychoanalysis, the analyst is paid to listen for the moments in which the Truth has a chance of emerging into the Real, and to encourage such moments. In writing, and indeed in all the arts, it is we who have to pay ourselves to recognise such moments and to elaborate them. But we also have to cancel and bin the empty words and gestures which rise up to blind us to such insights as it may be our good fortune to discover and rediscover on our creative journeys.

*

References

Atkinson, K. (1995) *Behind the Scenes at the Museum.* Doubleday

Barthes, R. (1972) 'Death of the Author', in *Image, Music, Text*, translated and edited S. Heath. Fontana

Barthes, R. (1982) *Camera Lucida.* Jonathan Cape

Freud, S. (1976) *The Psychopathology of Everyday Life*, translated and edited A. Tyson. Penguin

Giddens, A. (1979) *Central Problems in Social Theory.* Macmillan

Harré, R. and Madden, E. (1975) *Causal Powers.* Basil Blackwell

Kivy, P. (1980) *The Corded Shell.* Princeton University Press

Lacan, J. (1967) *The Language of the Self.* Johns Hopkins University Press

Phillips, A. (1993) *On Kissing, Tickling and Being Bored.*
Faber and Faber

Wilden, A. (1967) *The Language of the Self.* Johns
Hopkins University Press

Winnicott, D. (1971) *Playing and Reality.* Penguin

Wollheim, R. (1987) *Painting as an Art.* Thames and
Hudson

12

What is English if not a Language?

This chapter develops a distinction between language as something we have knowledge of and language as something we have beliefs about. This distinction is formulated using the philosopher's notion of an intentional object of belief. Together with the distinction between distributive (individual) intuitions and collective judgements (mutual beliefs), the argument seeks to dissolve false controversies between psychological and sociological approaches to the study of language. In his New Horizons in Language and Mind, *Noam Chomsky writes* "I know of only one attempt to come to grips with these problems," *citing earlier versions of this chapter as that attempt.*

*

I will go more or less straight to the point.

An anthropologist, whose male native informant claims to be the reincarnation of an eagle, will record the informant as *believing* that he is the reincarnation of an eagle, not that he *is* a reincarnation. But when the informant claims to be a native speaker of Hopi, the anthropologist will record him simply as a native speaker of Hopi. Anthropologists who are anthropological linguists will then to try to construct a grammar of Hopi. The problem which always arises is that no two informants' versions of Hopi are identical. Linguists have, historically, responded to this problem by reconstructing the concept of *a language* in diverse but generally unsatisfactory ways, surveyed in chapter 3 of my *Language in Mind and Language in Society*. The implausibility of these reconstructions, some of which bear all the fantastic hallmarks of attempts to save a discredited theory - for example, William Labov's probabilistic "community grammars" - ought to suggest that something is fundamentally wrong in the general strategy. And indeed it is. The cause of all subsequent difficulties is the initial assumption that if someone says they are a speaker of Hopi then, in a straightforward sense, they are. If we recorded the claim to be a speaker of Hopi in the same way as the claim to be a reincarnation of an eagle, the difficulties disappear. To turn the Eurocentrism of this paragraph round, imagine now a Hopi anthropologist studying people who claim to be speakers of English.

Let "S" designate any one of these people. Then for any S who claims to be a speaker of English (for simplicity, a native, monolingual, and male speaker), a first-shot revised anthropological transcription of the speaker's claim is represented by (1):

(1) S believes he is a speaker of English.

This is hardly exciting. It becomes so if you are prepared to grant that (2) represents the logical form of S's original claim:

(2) S believes, of the language he speaks, that it is English.

In philosophical terms, "English" appears in (2) as the intentional object of a speaker's belief and it appears opaquely: from the fact that some S believes he speaks English it does not follow that he believes he speaks Anglais, since he may not know that "Anglais" is the French word for "English." The belief he holds is opaque to whatever is the underlying reality; it is mediated by the way in which it is expressed. In contrast, "the language" appears extensionally and transparently in (2), so that if the language S speaks is actually (say) Jamaican creole, then we can substitute "Jamaican creole" or "créole de Jamaïque" for "the language" without affecting the truth of (2). There are many ways of thus designating what he speaks and none of them cloud the issue; they all aim at transparent identification. As this illustration suggests, the way things have now been reformulated allows that the language S speaks and S's beliefs about that language can vary independently of each other. This is a major theoretical claim and - I believe - a major gain. For it dissolves the linguist's problems with the "inherent variability of languages". The new formulation in (2) readily allows for the possibility that "the language he speaks" may vary from individual to individual – in the linguist's terms, it may always take the idiosyncratic form of an idiolect.

But, surely, it may be objected, there must be some connection - indeed, an intimate connection - between the language S speaks and his belief as to what it is, for otherwise we should expect to find cases like (3), but we don't:

> (3) S believes, of the French he speaks, that it is English.

Two comments.

First, it is by no means clear that we do not find cases

like (3). After all, it used to be commonly said that some children of West Indian origin encountered problems in the British educational system because though *they* thought they were speakers of English, their teachers didn't. Their teachers thought of them as speakers of creoles with insufficient resemblance to or mutual intelligibility with English to be counted as English. Viv Edwards did the research back in the 1970s.

Second, if you consider how, developmentally, speakers might acquire beliefs about which language they are native speakers of, it is intuitively obvious that they do not acquire them by inspecting the language they speak and matching it with samples of a named language, as if they were matching a colour to what it is called in a colour-sample book. Rather, they are told which language they speak in the context, for example, of over-hearing speakers of a foreign language for the first time ("They are speaking French. We speak English"). The belief is acquired on authority and is a mutual belief: I believe I am a speaker of English because you believe I am, and I believe you believe you are a speaker of English because ... and so on through as much embedding as your brain can handle. In other words, *speaking a language* and *getting to name what language it is that you are speaking* are quite separate activities.

Those two remarks made, it is nonetheless true that our language (or *knowledge of language* in Chomsky's phrase) and our beliefs about our language interact in complex ways. Without this interaction there would not be a politics of language – and there clearly is, as attested by the endless encounters between professional linguists and indignant guardians of language standards. These interactions require very careful mapping, but that is only to say that the intentionalist approach to languages

as objects of belief suggests a detailed research pro-
gramme in which linguists, psycholinguists and sociolo-
gists of language might be able to engage collaboratively
without promptly falling out with each other.

First, of course, speakers have many beliefs and mutual beliefs about language in general and their own language in particular, many of which will be well-founded
enough to allow them to be confident in guiding children
and foreigners to acceptable linguistic practice in a given
community. However, speakers are constantly liable to
over-confidence and also to mistaking the source of their
authoritativeness in any particular instance. Compare,
for example, my well-founded belief that in certain
cultural contexts it is not acceptable for would-be speakers of English to use double negation ("I haven't got no
money") with my intuition that (4) is ungrammatical:

(4) Who did you see the woman that met in town?

Now I am confident that readers of this chapter will
also judge (4) ungrammatical, but that does not entail
that we are bound together by cultural knowledge in the
form of mutual beliefs from which we authoritatively
judge the ungrammaticality of (4). For in this instance, it
is possible that we judge alike because (4) shows the
violation of a principle of universal grammar. I have
taken (4) from David Lightfoot's *The Language Lottery*,
where it is used to illustrate just that possibility. That we
then all judge each on our *own* authority (*distributively,*
as the philosophers say) that (4) is ungrammatical is
radically different from our judging *collectively,* as
members of a standard-setting normative community,
that double negation is unacceptable. In the former case,
our "judgement" is better described as an *intuition* which

provides indexical or symptomatic evidence about properties of some non-introspectible mental structure. We
either intuit that (4) is ungrammatical or we don't, and if
we do then in all likelihood we will not be able to
articulate why. In psychological experiments into human
vision, intuitions are commonly elicited which do not for
one moment commit those responding to a view about
what *others* should see, even though they may well
happen to see in exactly the same way. That is true of the
Müller-Lyer illusion, for example, where everyone sees
the lines with arrow heads as of unequal length. But they
are in no sense expressing a community or communal
view. In contrast to this sort of intuitive, distributed
consensus, judgement proper connects us through introspection with beliefs which are communal or shared, but
often also disputed. Sometimes there is consensus,
sometimes not and where not that indicates a fault line
in our language community.

In everyday practice we simply do not distinguish these
two sources of our authoritativeness - judgement and
intuition - and generally get along well enough without
doing so. In addition, and to make it worse, we are sometimes led to judge for others when we have no solid
ground either in introspectible shared beliefs or intuited
underlying structures. Thus, I well remember telling a
college student in Devon that he could not say "comprises
of," but only "is comprised of" or "comprises," only to be
confronted on next encounter with particulars from
every estate agent in town declaring that "the house
comprises of ....". Unwittingly, I had pitted my own
idiolect or dialect against local practice, the very error
against which professional linguists like Peter Trudgill
(in his *Accent, Dialect and the School* and elsewhere)
have rightly campaigned.

However - and this is the second point about interaction between *Knowledge of Language* and *Beliefs About Language* - what sustains those who make it their job to prescribe linguistic rules and practices against the onslaughts of the linguists is the fact that our (mere) beliefs about language can not only affect our speech and writings but also, through time, *enter into the grammar of the language we speak.*

In cases of what are called *hypercorrection* someone's speech is partly controlled by mistaken beliefs they hold about correct or proper or desirable speech forms. In England, Northerners know that Southerners pronounce "grass" with a glottal (throaty) *aaa*-sound and have sometimes thought, mistakenly, that the way to speak properly is to amend, *in every case*, their own native labio-dental /a/ to the glottal sound and thus end up saying "gaaas" for "gas." That does have unexpected consequences: when in 1961 I heard the northern minister in my southern Methodist church start telling a parable about *gaaas lamps*, I began to have teenage religious doubts.

Through time, practices like that just sketched and which for one generation are controlled by their *beliefs* about language can enter into the next generation's *knowledge* of language. This is because children do not hear that a particular piece of speech has been produced by a double process involving adaptation or hypercorrection of a native form; they hear only the *output*. The mental processes involved in generating that output are unobservable. Consequently, children may come to produce the final form without the mediation of conscious, belief-based adaptive or transfer rules: the term "adaptive rule" is due to the Danish linguist Henning Andersen; "transfer rule" to the British linguist, Richard

Coates. My three year old daughter used to say "he or she" when she didn't know the sex of a referent ("When our new baby is born, he or she will sleep in my room"). And her advantage over me was that she didn't have to employ an adaptive rule to produce this form since there was no earlier form which it replaced. I had been conscientious in adapting my speech when talking to her, but she may not have been adapting when talking to me.

I should add that I have no views on what policy to adopt in a language such as French which does have gender, *le bebé* being masculine. It is a matter of controversy among linguists what the relation is between grammatical gender (masculine, feminine) and sex (male, female). The difference is what allows people over there to say *J'éspère que le bebé sera une fille* [I hope that the baby will be a girl] without self-contradiction and explains how a French-speaking midwife making a special effort for expatriate English-speaking parents can end up declaring, in English, *He's a girl!* which perfectly illustrates the difference between *grammatical gender* and real-world *sex*.

Despite everything I have said, it is clear enough that the idiolects of speakers who believe themselves to be speakers of the same language do indeed cluster enough for that belief to be highly plausible. For most practical purposes, it is true that over there they speak French while over here we speak English. Some like Pierre Bourdieu would probably say that this clustering owes everything to the practices of modern national educational systems in reproducing national languages. This is the drift of his *Ce que parler veut dire.* Yet that is by no means self-evidently true, though it is partly true for languages like Swedish, Danish and Norwegian which have been deliberately developed away from each other.

But it may be that this clustering should sometimes be attributed to the operation of innate constraints on language development. Chomsky puts it this way in *Rules and Representations*:

I see no reasonable alternative to the position that the basic reason why knowledge of language comes to be shared in a suitably idealized population (and partially shared in actual populations) is that its members share a rich initial state, hence develop similar steady states of knowledge. (p.80)

Much work, especially in the mathematical theory of language learnability, has been devoted to fleshing out this claim, seeking to show how if the parameters of universal grammar are set in particular ways, specific language structures become intuitively (unreflectingly) accessible and preferred from a given linguistic starting-point input. Just as Google second-guesses with amazing prescience what we are trying to type, so universal grammar anticipates language structures on the basis of very limited evidence. But whatever isomorphism between speakers' *knowledge* of language and their *beliefs* about their language finally exists, it should not be allowed to obscure the major differences between these two orders of reality. The price of obscurity is that the arguments between professional linguists and grammar purists will remain at cross purposes.

*

References

Andersen, H. (1973) "Abductive and Deductive Change," *Language*, vol. 40, pp. 765 – 93.

Bourdieu, P. (1982) *Ce que parler veut dire*. Fayard

Chomsky, N. (1980) *Rules and Representations*. Oxford: Blackwell

Chomsky, N. (2000) *New Horizons in the Study of Language and Mind*. Cambridge University Press

Coates, R. (1982) "How Standard is Standard?" in Pateman, T. ed., *Languages for Life*, University of Sussex Education Area Occasional Paper 10, pp. 34 – 49.

Edwards, V. (1979) *The West Indian Language Issue in British Schools*. Routledge Kegan Paul

Johansen, J. and Sonne, H. (1986) *Pragmatics and Linguistics. Festschrift for Jacob L. Mey*. Odense University Press

Lightfoot, D. (1982) *The Language Lottery*. MIT Press

Pateman, T. (1987) *Language in Mind and Language in Society*. Oxford University Press

Trudgill, P. (1975) *Accent, Dialect, and the School*. Edward Arnold

Part Three

13

Never Mind. E. Weber
Love You Always

I<small>T</small>'s a beautiful line. John le Carré deploys it three times in *A Perfect Spy*. It aims straight at that desire for a love which is not just enduring but which was always-already there even before we were born and which will still be there when we are dead. We don't have to earn it and there is nothing which will cause us to forfeit it – no crime, no disloyalty, no neglect. Age does not wither it.

It's the kind of love you search for if you never had a good-enough father or good-enough mother to love you, and that is the situation of Carré's perfect spy, Magnus Pym. He never forgets the line and when he is reminded of it in the final days of his life, he weeps. It goes straight to the absences which both drive him and disable him.

The *Never Mind* is a phrase we have heard from our very earliest years - especially then - and so it sets up the line as an address from adult to child. But the adult does not identify as one normally would and instead uses this strange form *E. Weber*. The reader of the book, however, knows that E. Weber is female and that the night before writing her note, she has tried to seduce the teenage Pym. With the few written words which signal her disappearance, she also leaves enough money for him to escape from what passes as home in England.

The real cleverness of the line is in the way it is written by a foreigner, who is not word-perfect in English. A native speaker would have written *will love you always* or *will always love you*. The song which bursts forth with

I will always love you stumbles against the same defect
of grammatical correctness. These versions link love to
time and to will-power. The word *will* directs a gaze into
the future, forgetting that, often enough, it is the past
which is just as important. We don't want someone's
future love. We want someone's love which never had a
beginning and never has an end. The grammatically
correct version also hints at the possibility of a choice
since *I will* pairs in our minds with *I won't*. We most
definitely don't want a love which someone might be
choosy about. We want it unconditionally.

E. Weber's imperfect English allows her to escape both
limitations and thus, even without intending it, to speak
to Magnus Pym in the language of salvation. Her love
has no beginning and so no end. She just love you. She
has no choice, no reason. She just do.

*

10th Feb 2017

Dear Trevor Pateman,

Thank you so much for your letter,
and the thoughtful & delightful piece
that accompanied it. It's hard to
believe now, but E. Weber, under
another name, had a real place in my
life, & an exquisitely wicked one, but
it was left to me to coin the phrase on
her behalf. And your closing 'She just
do' is worthy of the lady at her

charming best. All in the present, as
you so rightly say, for who wants
future love? Who would ever honour
such a dubious cheque?
Thanks so much – with best wishes,

David Cornwell
(John le Carré)

*

Magnus Pym is holed up after being exposed as a double
agent, writing his life story - memoir and confession -
addressed to his son. There are perils in all such ventures,
even when undertaken in the absence of hot pursuers.
The obvious risks are memory failure and the curse of
hindsight. Then there is the temptation to be sentimental
about how we lived then or ironic about how unironic we
were in our youth, and both temptations - for different
reasons - may be irresistible. Le Carré does the irony
hilariously in an imagined exchange of *billets doux*
between the barely-teenage Magnus and the authentically
posh and far away Jemima Sefton Boyd, and does it again
for a still-virginal Magnus at Oxford.

If we are writing in the present about the past what we
write is always an echo, but an echo necessarily inflected
by the journey since travelled. There is a well-known
essay by the philosopher Thomas Nagel titled *What Is It
Like To Be A Bat?* Even when you have forgotten the
argument, you remember the striking title which is rich
enough to enable a reconstruction of what Nagel probably
said. When you attempt a memoir of childhood or youth,
you are always having to imagine what it was like to be

yourself then, and immediately hit upon the problem that
then you were another self whose outer life and inner life
you may have pretty much forgotten. It's hard to evoke
it for yourself and perhaps even harder to evoke it for
someone else, the listener or reader who may try to
engage with your words. But, of course, as we get older
we always look on the bright side and convince ourselves
that we can indeed convey a sense of what it was like to
be me then. I am sure I can do it but - it's true - only
ironically. I have read my Mikhail Bakhtin and know that
this is not some personal failing but could well be a
necessary feature of narrative reconstructions, like the
one which now follows.

*

Some young people don't know this, but those of my age
grew up at a time when governments made strenuous
efforts to discourage heterosexuality. Co-education
stopped at eleven, if not before, and certainly before things
got dangerous to morals. You were sent off to single sex
schools - in my case, a state grammar school - where you
could have wild crushes on those of the same sex but
would find it difficult to meet hormones of the opposite
sex unless some oblivious organisation put on a Disco with
inadequate policing. My Methodist church did it once. I
got my first kiss off Methodism but since the disco was
not repeated, I arrived at university never having had a
girlfriend. I now had two rooms of my own, an obvious
asset, but every college was single-sex and, worse, they
had settled themselves into a system which yielded six
boys to one girl. The private sector had seen a niche market
opportunity and established finishing schools and secre-
tarial colleges, in close proximity and for girls only. The

girls were supposed to find an undergraduate male with current hormones and future prospects and thus, thanks to the marriage which ensued, never actually need to secretary. Male students had mixed feelings about these girls on a far from secret mission who made up the numbers at unsupervised discos. There is a book to be written on the secret history of the University of Oxford.

In my first year, I finally got another stroke of luck. In Freshers' Week 1965, I had signed up to all kinds of organisation, including the Campaign for Nuclear Disarmament's youth wing YCND which, unusually, sought members from the Town population as well as among students. I joined for motives which were entirely political, but it was there a few months later and aged eighteen that I met a local girl of sixteen, mid-way through her A levels. We took to each other, but there were difficulties. Her mother had left home, she lived with her father and two younger brothers, and her father was rather strict. He wanted to meet me before consenting to her not coming home straight from school and so on, which - among other things - would reduce her availability to do household chores. The father worked on the shop floor of what was then a major car factory, out at Cowley.

So there came a day when I presented myself at a house in the industrial suburbs of Oxford and sat down to lunch. Polite conversation, etc. The two younger brothers grinned but said little. There was a goldfish tank next to the dining table and I gazed into it at awkward moments. Suddenly, the youngest boy - I guessed he was ten - plunged his hand into the tank, pulled out a wriggling goldfish, threw back his head, dropped it into his mouth, swallowed, and presented me with a closed-mouth smile and *fait accompli*. Silence. Four pairs of eyes on me. Four black faces. *Would you like to try?*

Well, No, I would not. But clearly a lot hangs on this. As a member not only of YCND but a supporter of the Oxford Committee for Racial Integration - another supporter, the father, now looking at me - must I prove my commitment to integration (which swallows two ways) by sampling this novel West Indian delicacy?

I look at the fish tank again and, with a sense of failure, decline.

Correct response. General relief – and the young boy can't wait to explain how he did it. We have carrots on our plates - I have been eating them without difficulty - and he has simply secreted a bit of carrot in his hand, adjusting its position as he pulls it out of the tank, shaking it vigorously and visibly to bring off his party trick.

So I passed the Test and we were allowed to meet, both of us new to boyfriend and girlfriend stuff, both of us awkward and with many Issues we didn't know how to deal with. I forget how long it lasted, but it was fraught. We did not find salvation.

*

Children have all the time in the world. Adults are often impatient to "move on". This is one way in which they can end up mis-matched. A child in distress, whether from physical injury or emotional upset, needs to be held. Sometimes the parent takes the initiative and embraces the child, sometimes the child clings to the parent. Distress in a child is often overwhelming, exacerbated by the child's awareness that they have lost it; lost self-control, self-possession.

It may take a child a long time to calm down and a good-enough parent will allow the child to feel that they are there for as long as it takes. It simply doesn't work to tell children to pull themselves together. Children know they should and know they can't. That's a large part of the distress.

It used to be standard in children's homes for staff to hold on tight to children in distress, children who were acting out - throwing things, attacking people. I don't know if staff are still allowed to do that; I hope so. Adults also need to be held and holding is one of the things lovers do for each other. There are symbolic forms of holding. The psychiatrist R D Laing somewhere gives an account of an analysis in which his patient sat silently. Laing responded in kind but got bored and tried to move on. He began to think about other things; probably he began to fidget. The patient finally broke the silence. *Don't leave me.* I doubt Laing was much surprised, nor would he have been puzzled by the idea that Magnus Pym, as Pym himself writes, *preferred to test the limits of the tolerance of those he loved.*

Children will let go when they have recovered. Made to let go too soon, they will cling. Rebuffed, they will eventually lose the capacity to be held and to hold. Later in life, sometimes we need to be held and sometimes we need to hold, to be saved or to save. As a young man, Magnus Pym needs to be held but cannot or won't readily acknowledge that. But E. Weber's promissory note is almost enough to satisfy his need and the cash in hand saves him in that practical way which is often salvation enough. Salvation is that much harder to find when there is a temporary problem of liquidity.

*

The gossip I overhear tells me that women often enough urge each other to get rid of the husband who is no longer

the man they married and they would be better off
without. Out of earshot, I guess that the powder room talk
is more cutting. Such talk does have real-world consequences: the overwhelming majority of divorces are
initiated by women who have decided to get rid. It's true,
of course, that the bastard may have already deserted.

Men rarely urge each other to get rid of the wife,
though they do commiserate with each other. For men,
exiting from marriage is not something collectively
planned in the locker room. It's a private crisis rather
than a public crusade. But it usually involves an enabler,
a helper – most often *The Other Woman*, who is never
a good fairy but always a wicked witch. Our folk tales
of marital break-ups are the only stories in which the
magic wand is wielded by a complete and utter villain.
As a result, real women often go to great lengths to avoid
the role of Other Woman; and, indeed, at times she has
been no more than a figment created to provide the fault
required by a divorce court. In spy fiction, she is
practised in the arts of entrapment and of lubricating
betrayal.

*

My own marriage - there was only one - was broken up
by the wand of someone who took a gamble and held
me. It was a warm day, a day for a walk. A park adjoined
the place where I worked and we went there. She had
told me something she had never told anyone and this
meeting was the follow up to discuss that disclosure.
But I also wanted to talk; I had secrets too. At the end,
she put her arms around me and hugged me. No adult
has hugged me like that for a very long time. I betray
and allow myself to be saved. The relationship lasts nine

years, more than long enough for creatures with seven ages and nine lives.

*

There is a young woman in tears in my sitting room. I know her a bit already and like her a lot. She's telling me about her situation and it's awful. So too is the loss of pride involved in telling anyone this story. She wants me to take her on. She tells me what she has in mind. For once in my life, I do not hesitate. I say I will, I do. I look after her for years and love the work of loving her. I'm good at the task I have been set.

She needs me to put her to sleep. I lie on my back, she pushes back her long black hair with a practised sweep, thumps her head into the socket of my neck and shoulder, and is secure for slumber. After an hour, the pain is excruciating. I dislodge myself, ease away, massage my neck, go to my own bed. She will sleep now till morning when I will go back and, almost without waking, she will lock down for another hour before the alarm separates us. I am the happiest man alive and I know it won't last. When the day arrives for us to part, we do not need to say very much. She just observes, to herself as much as to me, "I've grown up." Then we sit together silently, as they do in Russia at leave-takings with those who may not return for a long time, or ever. The relationship was quite unsuitable. There was beauty in that.

*

Saving and being saved. Such, if we are lucky, are the ways of salvation. None last forever, though many last longer than the Pym & Salvation Coach Company Ltd.

Undying love is a short-lived thing too, but not if it is brutally ended. Magnus Pym loses both his mother Dorothy and his beloved seducer Lippsie long before love can be put to the test of time and at such an early age that indelible shadows remain. E.Weber steps up with words which speak to the shadows. So too does Axel, code name Poppy, who Pym first betrays but who later becomes the indulgent controller of his double agent life. Pym is explaining himself when he writes of Axel that *He had to scold and forgive him like the parents who would never slam the door in his face.* And it is Axel, decades later and using his code name, who signs off with Elena Weber's words. As the fatal endgame approaches, he quotes them back to Pym concealed in a radio message that Magnus decodes in his last refuge:

He was weeping. He was laughing. He could scarcely read what he had written. NEVER MIND. E.WEBER LOVE YOU ALWAYS. POPPY.
'You cheeky sod,' he whispered aloud, punching away more tears. 'Oh Poppy. Oh my.'

*

Didn't care about money. Love was all he cared about. Didn't know where to find it. Clown really. Tried too hard says Sir Kenneth Sefton Boyd when quizzed much later in life about his old schoolmate. Maybe lasting salvation does come, but only to those who are free enough not to search for it.

14

Lost in The Credits

THIS is partly by way of explanation to my daughter Isabella whose company publishes my books. This is the fifth and, as she remarked, none of them have Dedications. The truth is I have gone off the genre. In my mind, dedications have merged with gravestones and I'm against those too. Too little and too late.

I can't think of a painting - though I am sure there is one - with a little box in one corner and the painted words, *To my wife who kept me in mugs of tea.* No, if painters want to show appreciation, they just paint you. And even if you don't make it into a big exhibition piece, they may make a little sketch and offer it you as a gift. Half a dozen words at the front of a novel seems a poor thing in comparison. If they can make them fit, writers can and do turn their family, friends and lovers into characters of the novel itself, but then - unlike painters - they usually disguise them. In imitation of what painters do, I did try my hand at writing extended pieces and giving them as presents to the adult individuals they portray. But only twice. Whether those pieces still exist depends on whether the recipients kept them.

I can think of two works of visual art which push the idea of Dedication to its limits. First, there is Tracey Emin's name-embroidered tent *Everyone I Have Ever Slept With 1963 – 1995,* though in fact she hadn't slept with all of them. Never mind. It's the thought that counts. The tent is a sort of memorialisation, the work exhausted in the act of dedication.

Then, back in the nineteenth century, there is Gustave Courbet's big painting *L'atelier du peintre*. We can imagine the crowd of people in the image as not really there all at the same time in the painter's studio but rather as the roll-call of those who had visited the *atelier* over the years, their relations to the painter very varied. This is not my own analysis of the painting; I owe it to Ruth Bernard Yeazell who develops the argument in her book *Picture Titles*.

Sometimes, a writer's dedication imposes an obligation. You hang a work around someone's neck and that entails that you can accuse them later of disloyalty: *I dedicated my novel to you, now look what you have done to me.* That reverses the original situation in which the obligation was imposed the other way, on the writer by the patron who expected to be memorialised and would feel betrayed if they were not.

There are other issues about form and content which interest me. There are the conventions about Acknowledgements which introduce bits which clunk into what might otherwise be a sleek machine. Twice now I've tried to write the acknowledgements into substantive chapters so that instead of stopping and changing mode, they are supposed to read as a continuation of the text. My starting point is the experience of going to the cinema, being moved by the film in such a way that at the end I just sit there, lost in the Credits as they scroll up the screen.

*

On Language In General begins with an improvisation on the view of language I develop in my entirely academic *Language in Mind and Language in Society* (1987). The letter from Lacan is dated 14 XI 71 and the postcard from Barthes 22 VII 75. Franz's initiative is credible because the real Freud was quite capable of giving advice when asked. One of my friends from that time in Paris, Sanda Geblesco, did go to talk to Lacan and the results have now been posthumously published as Elisabeth Geblesco, *Un amour de transfert* (2008).

Making It Up As You Go Along includes a story *It Was A Dark and Stormy Night* which in a slightly different version was published in *Pandora's Books,* edited by Richard Crane (1997). Allan Ahlberg had responded to the story in draft, giving me encouragement ("I like it – it's good." Letter of 23 November 1995). Names are borrowed from characters in Janet and Allan Ahlberg books, read to my children Isabella and Mitzi in the 1980s.

Playing a Bad Hand Well could lead on to *Matisse in the Studio*, edited by E McBreen and H Burnham (2017), to Leonard Cohen's extraordinary final album *You Want It Darker* (2016) and to the 1966 novel by Jean Rhys *The Wide Sargasso Sea*. At the last minute, there arrives John le Carré's *A Legacy of Spies* (2017).

I Can Write It and You Can Rhyme It owes to my friend, the late Selwyn Hughes who wrote under the name of Selwyn Pritchard and for some years ran a field centre in Orkney. Ann Jefferson told me to read *The Blue Flower*.

Prose Improvements uses first UK editions of the novels cited. I read the Suzanne Rindell interview at https://ravencrimereads.wordpress.com/2014/01/18/an-interview-with-suzanne-rindell-the-other-typist-blog-tour/. There are numerous academic studies of Free Indirect Discourse (which has several variant names). I

am relying on V N Volosinov *Marxism and the Philoso-
phy of Language* (Russian original 1929; first English
translation 1973); R Pascal *The Dual Voice* (1977); A
Banfield *Unspeakable Sentences* (1982). That is not an
exhaustive list of the relevant literature. I discuss the
topic in chapter 3 of my *Studies in Pragmatics* (2017).

How To Do Things With Commas gets its title from
J L Austin's *How To Do Things With Words* (1962), the
founding text of contemporary linguistic pragmatics.

Apostrophe's hopefully leaves you eager to go online for
more annoying Math problems. The sentence "See if you
can hum it while I play it." is the shortest summary I can
manage of R Lerdahl and R Jackendoff's *A Generative
Theory of Tonal Music* (1983).

Lost in Translation may be supposed allusive to the film
of the same title but since I thought the film really bad, I
don't think I can be alluding to it. I am just using a title
which fits what I am writing about. Agreed?

Ungrammarly alludes and the text itself includes reference
to an essay "Letters Not About Love" which appears in my
Silence Is So Accurate (2017), both titles appropriated, from
Viktor Shklovsky and Mark Rothko respectively.

Language and Identity Politics relies on various
sources, including Einar Haugen's "The Scandinavian
Languages as Cultural Artifacts" in his book *The Ecology
of Language* (1972).

**Writing: The Teachable and Unteachable in Creative
Writing** is revised from a version appearing in *The*

Journal of Aesthetic Education, volume 32, 1998, with copyright material re-used by kind permission of the Board of Trustees of the University of Illinois.

The Empty Word and the Full Word is extensively re-written from a version appearing in *The Self on the Page*, edited by Celia Hunt and Fiona Sampson (1998). Celia Hunt was my doctoral student, turning her thesis into *Therapeutic Dimensions of Autobiography in Creative Writing* (2000) which explores parts of the same territory as this chapter, but with Karen Horney as a theoretical guide.

What is English if not a Language? is revised from versions appearing in *Pragmatics and Linguistics: Festschrift for Jacob L. Mey* edited by J D Johansen and H Sonne (1986) and then in my *Language in Mind and Language in Society* (1987). Jacob Mey had been generous about my early work, reviewed it in *The Journal of Pragmatics* which he co-founded, and invited me to talk at Odense University where he taught. In that way, I came to be a contributor to a *Festschrift* which proved rather premature. He is still alive thirty years later. Noam Chomsky discusses my arguments in several essays and lectures, dating back to 1989, all a bit different but most accessibly in *New Horizons in the Study of Language and Mind* (2000) - go to the index - and most recently (2005) in "Construcciones mentales y realidad social," in CIC *(Cuadernos de Información y Comunicación)*, volume 10, pp. 47 – 83.

Never Mind. E.Weber Love You Always is indebted to David Cornwell for generous permission to use his letter to this author. The goldfish story is told with the knowledge of the girl at the lunch and her prankster brother. At the end, I adapt a line from Penelope Fitzgerald's *The Blue Flower* where in chapter 49 the Bernhard declares of his brother's proposed marriage *It is quite unsuitable ... it is our business to see the beauty of that.* Fitzgerald had a talent for spectacular one-liners. In her novel *The Bookshop* it is the narrator who delivers deadpan the observation that *morality is seldom a safe guide for human conduct.* I desperately wanted to sneak that into my text, but couldn't make it fit so I simply put it here.

Lost In The Credits is the chapter you are reading and which ends with Acknowledgements, going mainly to Fern Horsfield-Schonhut and Sîan Rees. From different backgrounds in language studies and historical writing, both editors suggested many changes and secured more than I would normally regard as reasonable. I am very grateful to them both.

Geoff Fisher is getting familiar with my hopes and hobby-horses; this is the fifth book he has typeset, helping to create an overall appearance with which I am very happy. Ilva Kalnberza is on her fifth book cover and has also helped give these books a house style. This time, the jacket uses a photograph I took after the hurricane which swept southern England in October 1987, leaving millions of trees uprooted and waiting for the chainsaw.

My daughter Isabella accepted the liability of publishing my books and I hope she will now find some more profitable titles to expand the **degree zero** imprint created out of Munken premium white, Times New Roman, Arial Black, Segoe Script, Wibalin and, last but not least, my exasperating friend Microsoft Word, Sisyphus to the end of the line.

Trevor Pateman

Work In Progress

The Unwilling Suspension of Belief

We start out in life believing everything. There are good reasons to think it could not be otherwise. We cannot begin with distrust or even suspension of commitment. To the youngest of young children, the world is as it seems and that means that when a story is read or a stage play performed, then those things can be as funny or scary as anything in everyday life. As a result, and quite often, an adult will end up trying to comfort with the words, "It's only pretend" — perhaps not realising that pretence is the very thing which needs to be understood.

It is by a very long and devious route that adults sometimes claim the ability to offer up a "Willing Suspension of Disbelief" (the phrase is due to S T Coleridge) when reading a novel or watching a film. I think they are deluding themselves. We never suspend disbelief, willingly or otherwise, because we never really disbelieve. We are natural believers – as makers of Fake News realise – and the only progress we make from our initial state of general belief is to develop a small ability to dodge belief, avoid whole-hearted commitment, when we encounter art or entertainment or serial liars.

Even then, the ability is very limited as authors of sentimental love stories and makers of frightening films know only too well. They need only a small bag of tricks to make us laugh, cry and feel fear because that is what we are born to do. Of course, we know "It's only a movie" but there is a great big chunk of our mind which doesn't know and which is very easy to tap into – quite often in ways we try to stop or ways to which we hate ourselves for succumbing.

"I know these are only words, but all the same" ... (I am moved as though these words were uttering a reality)

And that's someone who's supposed to be all against this way of thinking: Roland Barthes, in The Pleasure of the Text. You need no special endowment to be touched by works of art. You just need a bit of education – "It's only pretend" – in order not to be touched by them too much. Even then the education isn't very effective.

About the Author

Trevor Pateman was born in 1947 and after a grammar school education studied in Oxford, London and Paris. He has been publishing his writing since 1968 when after graduating with a congratulatory First, he wrote a critique of Oxford's PPE degree. His most cited academic work is an investigation and defence of Chomskyan linguistics, *Language in Mind and Language in Society* (Oxford University Press 1987). In recent years he has tried to move away from the academic style into more personal but still analytic writing, notably in *The Best I Can Do* (2016) and *Silence Is So Accurate* (2017).

He reviews books at **readingthisbook.com**